Recovering HOPE

Recovering HOPE

Science-Based Tools
for Long-term Healing from
Depression, Anxiety & Addiction

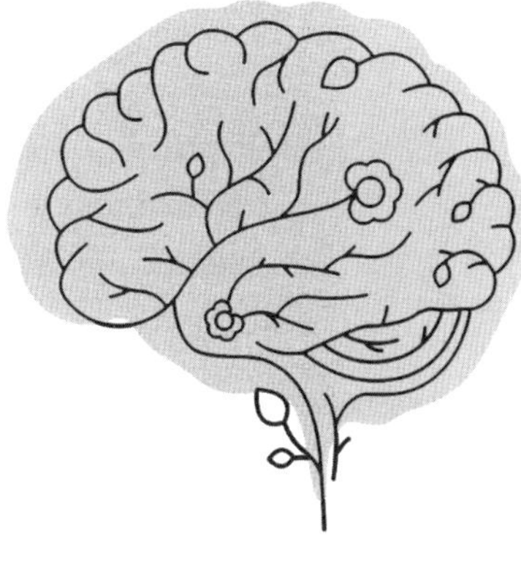

Clay Olsen & Jacob Z. Hess, PhD

Published by Familius LLC, www.familius.com
PO Box 1130, Sanger, CA 93657
Familius books are available at special discounts for bulk purchases, whether for sales promotions or for family or corporate use. For more information, contact Familius Sales at orders@familius.com.

Library of Congress Control Number: 2026941687

Print ISBN 9798893962017
Ebook ISBN 9798893962192

Printed in China

Edited by Gretchen Picklesimer Kinney and KaTrina Jackson
Cover design by Brooke Jordan
Book design by Maggie Wickes

10 9 8 7 6 5 4 3 2 1

First Edition

FSC www.fsc.org MIX Paper FSC® C188448

To Jen & Monique

"Courage doesn't always roar. Sometimes courage is the little voice at the end of the day that says I'll try again tomorrow."

—Mary Anne Radmacher

Foreword

As mental health professionals, we are often entrusted with the profound privilege of walking alongside individuals in their darkest moments. Through years of practice, I've seen the resilience of the human spirit—but also the heavy burden many carry when they're told their struggles are permanent. It's a message that, however well-meaning, can extinguish the faint flicker of hope that is so vital to recovery.

This is why *Recovering Hope* resonates so deeply with me. Clay Olsen and Jacob Hess offer more than a critique of the current mental health landscape—they offer a vision of transformation. Rooted in cutting-edge science, rich with real-life stories, and imbued with compassion, this book is a rallying cry for hope.

The authors challenge the narrative that mental illness is an unchangeable fate. Instead, they illuminate a path of possibility: one where neuroplasticity, lifestyle changes, and mindfulness create tangible, lasting healing. Their approach combines the rigor of research with the warmth of lived experience, making this work both intellectually sound and profoundly humane.

In my three decades of clinical practice, I've too often witnessed diagnostic labels become self-fulfilling prophecies. When we tell someone they have a "lifelong condition," we may inadvertently close doors that should remain open. Clay and Jacob boldly question this paradigm, not through wishful thinking but through examination of the landscape of research that points toward the brain's remarkable capacity for change.

What makes this book particularly valuable is its accessibility. They neither oversimplify the journey nor overcomplicate the science. Instead, they strike that delicate balance that makes transformation feel within reach for those who have long believed it impossible.

As you delve into these pages, you will encounter a wealth of insight—for instance, about how sleep, sunlight, nutrition, and connection can become tools of recovery. But perhaps most importantly, you will rediscover the power of hope. Hope that brighter days lie ahead. Hope that healing is not just possible but achievable.

The stories shared within—of individuals who reclaimed their lives despite receiving serious diagnoses—are not merely inspirational; they are instructive. They demonstrate patterns of recovery that challenge our most fundamental assumptions about the nature of mental illness. These healing narratives deserve our attention not because they are exceptional, but because they bring to light possibilities that have been systematically overlooked.

For anyone navigating their own journey or supporting someone they love, this book offers a new perspective: that tomorrow can indeed be better than today. As professionals, as friends, as family members, let us carry this message forward, creating spaces where hope is not just permitted but cultivated.

Clay and Jacob's work has profoundly influenced how I think about mental health—and I trust it will do the same for you. Their courage in questioning established paradigms, their commitment to evidence-based optimism, and their compassion for those struggling make this book not just a valuable resource but a necessary one in our current mental health landscape.

With admiration for their vision and gratitude for their courage,

—Mark Chamberlain, Ph.D.
Licensed Clinical Psychologist, Clinical Director at Suncrest Counseling

Preface

You know when you find something you love—an incredible restaurant, an amazing movie, or the perfect song that sums up your deepest emotions—and you just have to share it with someone?

That's why we wrote this book! The ideas, possibilities, research, and stories gathered in this book—all related to deep and lasting healing from emotional and behavioral problems—are as jaw-droppingly beautiful to us as a sunset . . . an uplifting vista that most people have never seen, though. This is our attempt to change that.

It's more than just the beauty of these ideas that motivates us, however. We also know too many beautiful people whose lives have been overcome by crippling depression, anxiety, and addiction, and who, we are confident, could be helped by what we've learned and seen in our work over the last decade.

In the summer of 2010, I (Clay) met Jacob at a conference in Utah focused on educating the public about the social harms of pornography. Jacob had just completed his doctorate in community psychology from the University of Illinois and had his eye out for public health approaches to depression, anxiety, and addiction. I was there at a booth representing Fight the New Drug, a nonprofit I cofounded in 2009 with a few friends to raise awareness about the harmful effects of pornography. Fight the New Drug was unique in that we were a youth-led movement that was based on science, facts, and personal accounts, as opposed to any religious or political ideation. We wanted to disrupt the standard approaches to this subject and help young people, especially, consider the risks before consuming.

On one particular spring morning, I was presenting to a group of middle school students during an assembly. I noticed in the front row a girl, probably 12 years old, watching intently and nodding her head at every major point. As soon as the presentation was over, the principal stood up and gave instructions on filing out of the gymnasium to their next class. This young girl broke away from her group and ran up to me as I was packing up. With tears welling up in her eyes, she said, "I just wanted to say thank you for your message. I have been struggling with pornography in my own life for a while now, and I just haven't known what to do about it. I now feel like I can overcome this."

I was already aware by then that today's youth were dealing with this challenge like no other generation before. But it really struck me to have an innocent twelve-year-old tell me—within earshot of her peers—that she had been struggling.

This, along with countless other experiences, inspired me to develop a free online program, called Fortify, to help people both young and old overcome a struggle with sexual compulsivity. I knew that the available options at the time required both parental consent and a credit card, which for many teens was a Mount Everest they were unable or unwilling to climb. I immediately called Jacob and asked if he would ever consider joining us full-time, explaining our hopes and ambitions for the project.

Jacob and I joined forces for the next decade. His academic background complemented my entrepreneurial and grassroots approach. We began working with clinical professionals and industry leaders from around the globe, and over the years, we visited and heard from tens of thousands sharing their stories with us.

Jacob had studied depression for his dissertation, interviewing people to understand what long-term outcomes look like. Eventually, we began expanding our focus beyond sexual compulsivity to address broader mental health concerns.

That is when Impact Suite was born, a modern mental wellness company getting at the roots of emotional health through preventative technology and professional care. Jacob and I, along with our amazing Impact Suite team, have continued to work together to develop innovative approaches to mental health care—reaching hundreds of thousands from around the world.

We started this journey with a desire to make the greatest difference possible—swinging the metaphoric sledgehammer as strongly as we could for good. Along the way, we've marveled at the courage of so many who are grappling with their own crippling fear and despair as well as many kinds of suffocating addictions.

That includes people we know and love—witnessing close-up in our own friends, family members, neighbors and coworkers the agonizing day-by-day struggle that serious mental and behavioral problems can often entail.

Over this time, we've also met many caregivers and mental health professionals who have been "in the trenches," doing everything they can to make a difference with so much skill and compassion.

As you read through these pages, you'll find not just the culmination of our professional collaboration but also a distillation of our shared passion from the last decade for reaching people who are tempted to give up hope and giving them a reason to keep going. Our journey from addressing pornography addiction to tackling broader mental health issues through Impact Suite reflects our commitment to empowering individuals to find greater hope, healing, and happiness.

Our hope and sincere prayer is that this book will boost the spirits of those who are currently holding on with their fingernails emotionally, and the wonderful people supporting them too. Based on the stories, experiences, and research we've witnessed over the last decade, one thing has become abundantly clear: Tomorrow *doesn't* have to be the same as today.

There is peace, happiness, and healing out there beyond your wildest imagination.

Even if you can't feel that right now, are you open to feeling that one day soon? "There's a big difference between some hope and no hope," one woman told us.

Even just a spark of hope can illuminate the darkest path. Throughout this book, you'll meet people who once stood exactly where you stand now—people who couldn't imagine ever feeling better—who have found their way to genuine healing and joy. Their journeys weren't always easy, but they're proof that your story isn't over yet. Brighter days truly are ahead.

Contents

Introduction

What's darker than depression, scarier than anxiety, and more oppressive than addiction?

Being told you'll never overcome what you're facing. And, in the middle of your deepest pain, becoming convinced that this is the hard truth about your life and future.

Sadly, that's more or less what many people have been encouraged to believe: "Once an addict, always an addict"; "Your brain has a permanent chemical imbalance"; "This is something you'll deal with for the rest of your life."

Even if well-intentioned, these messages can multiply discouragement enormously—with people persuaded that there's no lasting healing to be found from the agonizing anxiety, the consuming despair, or the crippling craving. No, they've just lost the genetic lottery, so their unlucky minds and lives will always be a twisted maze without an exit.

The story we've been told about mental health problems—that they are permanent chemical imbalances requiring lifelong management—is fundamentally incomplete. A growing body of evidence reveals that what we experience as depression, anxiety, and addiction has far more to do with our lives, environments, and histories than it does with permanent biological defects. This paradigm shift opens up possibilities for genuine healing that go far beyond symptom management.

Treatment Instead of Healing?

Of course, no one—professional or otherwise—wants to leave people discouraged. We believe everyone is doing the best they can to alleviate suffering. Yet, despite billions of dollars spent on intervention and treatment—including easier access to a greater variety of medications, and more therapists per capita than at any other time in human history—rates of addiction, anxiety, depression, and suicide have risen to historic levels.

This isn't simply about more awareness leading to more diagnoses. It's more than that. And we're among the growing number who believe it's time to show more curiosity and courage in rethinking what we've been doing and how we've been approaching it—starting with the messages we send vulnerable people every day.

If science confirmed that these kinds of emotional and behavioral problems *really were* lifelong chronic conditions, then we *should* be upfront with people about that—helping them accept hard realities and do their best to cope with as much bravery as they can muster.

But that's just the thing—this *isn't* what the available science suggests at all, which is so much more hopeful than people realize.

In fact, the best research shows that anxiety, depression, and addiction have more to do with the details of our lives (past trauma and present lifestyle) than they do with biological predispositions alone (which can still play a role). More and more, we are recognizing that past experiences can leave us with unique vulnerabilities emotionally, while our current environment adds further emotional vulnerabilities in literally hundreds of potential ways.

Don't let that discourage you, though, because it's actually a *hopeful* message. If there are hundreds of contributors to emotional and behavioral struggles, that means there are also hundreds of things we can do about them. For instance, if you realize that too much stress or too little sleep are impacting you emotionally, those are areas of your life that you can change. And if you discover a little more sunlight, stillness, spirituality, or green vegetables could make a measurable difference for your mood, wouldn't leaning into that more be worth a shot?

We've seen this kind of hope and empowerment rekindled on a daily basis, over the last decade, in the lives of many people we've tried to support with our technology—not because they believed some theoretical promises, but because of concrete improvements they see happening in their own lives.

Far from wishful thinking, a pet philosophy, or naïve optimism, we'll make the case in subsequent chapters that this represents a legitimate, game-changing paradigm shift reflected in cutting-edge neuroplasticity (the changeable brain) and epigenetics (the fluid genome), along with outcome studies of mental health interventions involving micronutrients, physical activity, mindfulness, spirituality, and trauma healing.

Why This Matters

This isn't just an academic debate. The story we believe about our mental health shapes our expectations, our treatment choices, and ultimately our outcomes. If you believe you're permanently broken, you'll seek only to manage your condition. But if you recognize the many factors influencing your mental well-being, you open the door to deeper healing through changes within your reach. For too many people, the message to expect permanent illness has extinguished the hope needed to persevere through the healing process. It's time for a more complete story.

Many Contributors, Many Choices

Many people still don't realize there is a wide array of contributors to our mental and emotional state. Nor do they appreciate what this means for the future.

This puts the ball in your court. If we've been conditioned to struggle, that means we can be unconditioned. We can counteract vulnerabilities through small lifestyle adjustments over time that have proven to gradually improve our well-being.

Research backs this up: Even shifting one key lifestyle factor can lead to measurable reductions in mental health challenges and addictive behaviors (we know because we've measured that ourselves across many people).

That's true of shifting your diet, starting to meditate, getting some more physical activity, or going to bed a little earlier. There are similarly encouraging findings on sunlight, stress levels, level of connection, spirituality, meaning, and purpose.

But when you combine these factors, it gets even more exciting. A concerted set of small adjustments to key lifestyle categories has been shown to lead to improvements in mental health that are dramatic—and which don't just go away either.

Bottom line, even though so many aspects of our society set us up to struggle with mental health and addiction, there is so much more we can do in our own lives and homes to cultivate lives of sweetness and calm. We will show you how to uncover your own unique risk factors that can guide you towards gentle, gradual, targeted lifestyle changes. You can know for yourself, from watching your own life, that wonderful improvements, emotionally and behaviorally, are possible.

Small changes in one area can also spark changes in another. Neuroscientist Alex Korb writes that "one small change at a time" can reverse the course of depression and other emotional struggles by creating an "upward spiral." As he explains:

> In complex systems like the brain, even a little shift can change the resonance of the whole system. For example, exercise changes the electrical activity in your brain during sleep, which then reduces anxiety, improves mood, and gives you more energy to exercise [and interact with others]. Similarly, expressing gratitude activates serotonin production, which improves your mood and allows you to overcome bad habits, giving you more to be grateful for. Any tiny change can be just the push your brain needs to start spiraling upward.[1]

Imagine a mental health system centered on this kind of learning and growth—accepting whatever relief conventional treatments can provide, while reaching for deeper, more sustainable healing day by day.

That's our vision—dreaming of people currently grappling with substance abuse, sexual compulsivity, debilitating depression, and relentless anxiety regaining fresh hope that this *isn't* how their life has to always be. For well over a decade now, through our work at Fight the New Drug, Fortify, and Impact Suite, we've been gathering stories of people who have found deep and lasting healing from depression, anxiety, and addiction after years of struggle. Later in the book, we'll share our results (chapters 4 through 6).

First, we need to spend a little time outlining why a mental health paradigm shift is so needed (chapter 1) and what exactly that would look like (chapter 2). We'll then summarize the scope of literally thousands of studies in many areas that bolster hope in the possibility of deep and lasting emotional healing (chapter 3).

What This Book Does—and Doesn't—Address

The research, stories, and principles in this book focus primarily on depression, anxiety, and addiction. While other conditions like cancer and heart disease have long and encouraging histories of lifestyle change research, the research is still emerging on other mental health conditions.

While there may be some overlapping applicability to other conditions, we want to be clear: We aren't claiming here that these shifts will impact all mental health conditions equally. Conditions such as schizophrenia, bipolar disorder, and certain other diagnoses involve different biological mechanisms and environmental influences, which may call for different interventions. While the lifestyle principles we discuss—good sleep, nutrition, connection, and purpose—can offer valuable complementary support for anyone, we're not suggesting people should turn away from other medical treatments they've found helpful.

For anyone navigating a condition beyond the scope of this book, it can be valuable to work with qualified professionals who understand the unique needs of that situation. And take heart—there are many paths toward a meaningful life. Near the end of the book, we'll highlight steps you can take to cultivate an emotionally healing atmosphere in your own home, workplace, and community (chapters 7 through 9).

As you consider new steps on your own healing journey, don't be surprised if some turbulence arises. Deep and lasting healing is an adventure and quest you embark on, far more than a "just add water" recipe.

Setbacks of various kinds can keep you from who you want to become. So remember not to allow those discouraging moments to define you or to stop your progress.

You have infinite worth—and a future that is incredibly exciting.

Thank you for trusting us, at least enough to hear us out.

You won't regret it.

Part I

Why Do We Need a New Approach to Mental Health?

Chapter 1

Why Do We Need a Paradigm Shift?

Something isn't working in our approach to mental health. Despite unprecedented resources, expanding treatment options, and growing awareness, people are struggling more than ever. The time has come for a fundamental rethinking of how we understand and address emotional suffering.

In 1962, Thomas Samuel Kuhn, one of the most influential philosophers of science in the twentieth century, published one of the most highly cited academic books of all time: *The Structure of Scientific Revolutions*. Kuhn's groundbreaking thesis challenged the conventional view of science as a linear, gradual accumulation of knowledge. He suggested, instead, that scientific progress more often involves surprisingly abrupt changes in fundamental worldviews, which he called "paradigm shifts."[1]

This kind of disruption, however, hardly ever occurred during normal times when dominant paradigms were rarely questioned. Kuhn pointed out that the scientific community usually had to be pushed by a time of crisis toward fundamental revolutions in thought. In that kind of naturally disruptive period, new possibilities could arise as existing understandings failed to account for serious concerns.

Sound familiar?

A Crisis That Keeps Getting Worse

Rates of suicide, depression, and anxiety are reaching record highs both in the US and globally, despite enormous and ongoing efforts by scientists, practitioners, and policymakers. Today, the incidence of depression is approximately ten times higher than it was two generations ago—with evidence of generational worsening.[2]

The 29 percent of US adults reporting depression in a 2023 Gallup survey was the highest ever recorded by the organization[3]—10 percentage points higher than 2015, eight years earlier. Suicide, anxiety, and various kinds of addictions have also increased markedly in recent decades.

These aren't just statistics—they represent real human suffering. Behind each percentage point are millions of individuals experiencing profound emotional pain that can affect every aspect of their lives. Many people describe their depression as an all-consuming darkness that makes even the simplest daily tasks feel impossible.

Worse Even with Historic Efforts

Given the enormous investment in mental health over the last two decades, one would think these worrisome trends would have improved. Yet despite a more than 500 percent increase in antidepressant usage over the last decade and the highest number of therapists per capita in history, mental health struggles in developed Western countries are on the rise—especially for young people today.

According to a 2021 study by the US Centers for Disease Control and Prevention (CDC), approximately one in four teenage girls in the US seriously considered attempting suicide (a number that jumps to one in three for girls aged 14 to 18). This same report found the prevalence of suicidal thoughts among teenage American girls had increased from 19% in 2011 to 30% in 2021.[4]

Even with earnest and repeated professional efforts to improve mental health, many suffering people find themselves in a state of heightened despair—having "tried everything" to no avail.

Instead of investigating more carefully why these treatments are failing, however, all too often the attention goes to uncovering more layers of pathology in the person—with some individuals told they are "treatment-resistant," which signals that "even the best treatments don't work for you, that's how sick you are!"

So, what's really going on? In addition to a historic expansion of access to mental health treatments, technological advances around us suggest that human beings should be happier than in earlier eras . . . So, why aren't we?

Clues from Where You'd Least Expect

As you might expect, the answer to that question is not so simple—with wide disagreement existing in the research community. However, there are some clues that have been around for decades now, thanks to some fascinating anthropological studies of unique cultures.

Between 1966 and 1968, Dr. Edward Schieffelin lived among the Kaluli people in the rain forests of the Great Papuan Plateau in Papua New Guinea. Among other things, he wanted to know to what degree a group of people completely detached from our modern ways of living would struggle with depression.

"Despite living very hard lives," he later reported, "with none of the material comforts or medical advances we take for granted—*clinical depression is almost completely nonexistent*—with only 1 person in over 2,000 interviews who came close to meeting diagnostic criteria for depression."[5]

Did you catch that? Not one person in over 2,000 met the diagnostic criteria for depression. This is unheard of in modern American surveys.

In fairness, the sixties were quite a while ago, and it may be tempting to see these as historical differences rather than cultural ones. But cross-cultural research on other communities, including the Thai-Lao of Thailand[6] and the Toraja of Indonesia[7], confirms depression is rare among those who live furthest away from modernity.

And when they come closer to modernity, this uniqueness

dissipates. The hunter-gatherer Ik tribe of Uganda saw depression increase as they adopted more agricultural practices.[8] The same trend was observed in indigenous people in the far northern parts of the world, which saw a tripling of the suicide rate when they modernized.[9]

Reflecting on these findings, physician Brandon Hidaka writes in "Depression as a Disease of Modernity" that contrary to so many years of history, humans have dragged their bodies "into an overfed, malnourished, sedentary, sunlight-deficient, sleep-deprived, competitive, inequitable, and socially-isolating environment with dire consequences."[10]

By contrast, Dr. Stephen Ilardi from the University of Kansas points out that the more traditional ways of living are characterized by extensive physical activity, ample exposure to sunlight, and a diet rich in omega-3s—all of which have been confirmed in modern science as potent factors in combating depression.[11]

Little wonder, then, that at least *one* group in America hasn't been consumed by this epidemic of mental health problems: the Amish. Yes, the community famously mocked for living a very different lifestyle might have something to teach us.

Relax, we're not saying you have to "live like the Amish" in order to overcome depression. We're saying it might be good to live *a little more* like the Amish . . . for all of us!

Will More of the Same Ever Be Enough?

Whatever you think of that unusual advice, you'd have to agree that a call to lifestyle renovation is a far cry from what most people grappling with mental health challenges are hearing today.

Over the last two decades, our societal response to the widening epidemic of depression and anxiety seems to be, "If we're not seeing the results we want, let's take everything we've been doing . . . but *do it more.*"

The novelist Rita Mae Brown wrote in 1983, "Insanity is doing the same thing over and over again, but expecting different results."[12]

Yet it's important to remind ourselves that when people are in deep emotional pain, it's only understandable that they're willing to do anything they can to seek relief. One woman we interviewed compared her experience facing depression with her prior experience of being physically abused as a child. As she summarized:

> I've had beatings to the point of unconsciousness—ripped, broken, arms taken out of the socket and that compares nothing to the pain [of depression] that became every day, just right here [pointing to her chest]—this thing that wouldn't come off, that made it hard to breathe . . . like, I would rather have had hours and hours of people beating the crap out of me every day than to have been where I was just inside. It hurt that bad. There were times I thought it would kill me all on its own—that I wouldn't have to do anything.

When you're feeling emotional pain like this, anything to help manage or cope with the pain would naturally make sense. That is, after all, how many compulsive-addictive patterns start—as an unwise way to reach for some other way to feel better.

The real question is whether our efforts to *make feelings change* are actually working. It's well known that drugs, alcohol, pornography, and other addictive pathways don't end well, even if they start off providing some relief.

When it comes to legally prescribed psychiatric medication for depression and anxiety, many find initial relief from their emotional distress.[13]

Ultimately, however, that relief often starts to fade. A year or two later, many who initially found short-term reprieve with medication can sometimes experience an even greater emotional burden than before. That's not just our opinion. It's the conclusion of more than twenty different studies exploring long-term trajectories of conventional antidepressant treatment.

Yet, there's been surprisingly little attention to possible inadvertent consequences of our status quo approach, especially over the long-term. At the very least, then, the long-term evidence for conventional treatment that does exist would encourage caution. And international research over the last decade also confirms the wisdom of thinking twice.[14]

This isn't to suggest that medication has no place in treatment. For many people, medication can provide critical stabilization and relief. The key question is whether our almost exclusive focus on symptom management through medication and brief therapy is sufficient for long-term healing—and if paying more attention to underlying factors that may be fueling the epidemic of emotional distress could unleash more of that healing for everyone.

Once again, even a little relief can be worth celebrating when someone is feeling horrible. But we can become so focused on the prospect of bringing people this kind of a reprieve that we forget to ask this other important question: What does it take to experience more lasting relief from depression, anxiety, and other serious emotional distress?

And what if, instead of doing the same thing more and more, we could be doing something *new* that's proven consistently to yield very different results?

Looking to Longer-Term Hope

We're among the growing chorus of voices proposing a critical reevaluation of our approach to mental and behavioral health care—and encouraging consideration of a fundamental paradigm shift in how we understand and treat mental health disorders.

The reality is that many Americans have become so accustomed to sickness that they can hardly imagine a community where emotional illness isn't endemic. Yet, we've witnessed so many encouraging examples of families and communities learning for themselves how to effectively neutralize modern conditions that exacerbate depression, anxiety, addiction, and other related challenges.

We believe it's time to listen carefully to those raising serious questions about existing approaches, along with the many diverse voices pointing to fruitful alternatives. If we simply continue down the current path, let's not be surprised when worrisome numbers continue to worsen.

Everything depends on catching a vision as to why these changes need to be made in the first place. If you don't believe healing is possible, there is no way you'll even attempt such a change.

This book isn't about offering a magic bullet or promising easy solutions to complex problems. Rather, it's about expanding possibilities—about considering a broader range of factors that influence our emotional well-being, and exploring evidence-based approaches that address those same factors. It's about moving from a paradigm focused primarily on managing symptoms to one focused on proactively creating conditions for even more genuine healing.

So, let's grab the bull by the horns and talk about what a new paradigm shift in mental and behavioral health would look like—and how it could help move many more suffering individuals and families towards deeper, more lasting healing.

Chapter 2

Beyond Our Depressing Story about Depression

So, what exactly is the old mental health paradigm—and how precisely does it need to change? Have you ever heard someone say that they experience depression due to a chemical imbalance in the brain? It's part of a common belief in the permanence of emotional struggle.

When asked about her son, one woman told us, "There is no cure. He needs to learn to live with it the best he can. His brain is wired in a way that his mental illness will be a monkey on his back the rest of his life." Another individual shared that upon getting diagnosed, she was told that her "depression would be a lifelong condition."

What a depressing story we tell about depression. A teenager we know was diagnosed with depression at the age of sixteen and was told that she would deal with it for the rest of her life. As discouraging as this sounds to many of us, this is still a common way depression and other mental health conditions are talked about in medical schools, health books, medication advertisements, and other mental health classes[1]—lifelong and chronic, "like diabetes."

Only it really isn't. The neuroscience evidence doesn't back up that theory anymore. Yet, if people are being told this *is* the truth, it's no wonder why so many lose hope. In what follows, we will take this popular view of mental health and put it under a microscope—breaking down its core beliefs—which still inform so much of mental health care today. This includes convictions like:

1. **Intrinsic dysfunction:** The root cause of depression, anxiety, and other conditions is some kind of inherent brain problem, such as enduring deficiencies in chemical levels like serotonin.
2. **Long-term illness:** It's the nature of mental illness to be chronic. These challenges are lifelong conditions like severe physical disorders.
3. **Lifelong management:** The best thing we can do for people facing these problems is to provide tools to help them manage and cope—so they can learn to live as best they can with this "disability."

Naturally, any and all of these convictions can feel discouraging—lining up as they do with something found by Dr. Martin Seligman, the psychologist famous for introducing "learned helplessness" to the world. In one study, Seligman outlined three key characteristics that differentiate between whether a person sees the world with optimism or pessimism:[2]

1. **Personalization:** Seeing deficiencies as coming from inside oneself, rather than meaningfully connected to the circumstances of our lives—*I'm just messed up.*
2. **Permanence:** Believing that difficulties will largely remain unchanged throughout one's life—*It's always going to be this way.*
3. **Pervasiveness:** Considering difficulties as permeating all areas of life—*Everything is awful.*

These characteristics map remarkably well with the predominant American narrative of depression and other mental health challenges: Rooted internally in the brain, enduring throughout the lifespan, and touching virtually every aspect of life.

Jacob, one of the authors of this book, began paying attention to this narrative pattern after starting a study of depression over 20 years ago.[3] Among other things, one particular finding stood out: Above and beyond the acute, raw pain of depression, those suffering seemed to be carrying another kind of burden—one arising from the beliefs and interpretations many held *about* depression—what it was, where it came from, and what their future would be.

After touching on each of these common beliefs held by people facing mental health challenges, we'll turn briefly to some alternative views that could take their place—and why we should consider moving decisively in that direction.

Intrinsic Dysfunction—"Just How My Brain Is."

Perhaps the most noticeable feature of our Western mental health narrative is the belief that emotional pain arises largely (and almost unilaterally) from one's internal physiological make-up—a body that is fundamentally deficient, disordered, or defective in some way.

For at least a decade, up until the turn of the century, many brain scientists believed a "chemical imbalance" might explain what was happening. While there's no question configurations of chemicals play an ongoing role in our mental health, current neuroscience understandings have gone far beyond those early hypotheses.

This was underscored by a seminal 2022 review of the available serotonin research by scholars at the University College London.[4] After looking at patterns across 17 serotonin research studies, involving more than 164,000 participants, they concluded that there was "no support for the hypothesis that depression is caused by lowered serotonin activity or concentrations."

This groundbreaking study sent ripples through the scientific community, yet many clinicians continue to explain depression to patients using the chemical imbalance theory.[5] Why? Partly because simple explanations are comforting in the face of complex suffering, and partly because this narrative has become so deeply embedded in our cultural understanding of mental health that it persists despite contrary evidence.

Despite this absence of evidence, however, this belief has persisted for three decades—influencing the way so many people today make sense of their emotional struggles. One individual we spoke with defined depression as "that little glitch in my brain that doesn't produce the chemical that lets me be happy and content."

There's evidence to suggest that those who embrace a view of their own brain as deficient end up seeing their own prognosis as worse and feeling more pessimistic about the potential role of other non-medical treatments.[6] Mindfulness teacher Thomas McConkie once recounted a professional telling him that his "brain was like a car engine without oil."[7]

"I remember feeling dismayed," recalls Thomas, "a little bit crushed that all of a sudden this brain that had made such a good companion to me for sixteen years of my tender life, that it was deficient, that it was kind of broken." Rather than this being simply a "tough go at it," or "just this season of challenge and unrest," this teenager was left with the impression that "this is your brain, kid—this is how things are going to be." He admits, "I was upset; I felt deeply saddened by that prospect."

Dr. Elisha Goldstein, author of *Uncovering Happiness: Overcoming Depression with Mindfulness and Self-Compassion*, told us that "Our brain really runs us in a lot of ways. And if something's defective about it and we can't change it, that would make it difficult for someone to feel a lot of hope."[8]

We spoke with neuroscientist Amishi Jha at the University of Miami, who agreed: "If someone didn't understand that the brain is capable of changing, it could leave you in a very suffocating, constrained feeling."

Long-Term Illness—"Just How My Life is Going to Be."

If we've become persuaded that permanent internal deficiency lies at the heart of depression, it's unsurprising we would also see the illness itself as fairly enduring. In Jacob's earlier depression study, he asked participants, "Do you ever talk about 'getting better' from depression?"

One woman said, "I don't think that's possible," although she had wanted that. She said a couple years ago, she realized she was just "always going to have to deal with it." Another woman said, "They told me in the beginning [recovery] wasn't possible, but I'm hoping that I can make improvements that are permanent."

Jacob followed up by asking, "Who told you that you can't ever get better?" The woman responded, "Well my initial diagnosis—they said this is something permanent. They told me, 'This isn't something that you'll ever not have.'"

"The doctors all through, had all said that this was something that was chronic," another person recounted. "That as I got older, it would get worse."

Parents are often told similar things about children who are just starting their lives. One parent of a sixteen-year-old girl facing emotional challenges told us: "You bring them home from the hospital, nurse them, and dream that they will be successful . . . but then they come down with a mental illness that is there to stay lifelong. Your hopes and dreams die away."

Dreams and hopes of your child's future dying? Where are parents learning this?

What's particularly troubling is how this narrative contradicts solid epidemiological research showing that many people who experience depression do recover over time.[9] Rather than being the exception, recovery is actually the rule—yet this message rarely reaches those who need it most.

If you've really become convinced that there is no possibility of healing for your child, and that you're witnessing the beginning of a lifelong condition, does that sound like a mentality positioned to lead young people to deeper healing and a happy future?

Needless to say, this belief can be pretty discouraging to those who embrace it without question. One woman, Catherine, after experiencing profound healing from painful mental illness told us, "When you are already feeling hopeless and in despair, to have someone tell you that what you have is a condition that you're going to have to live with the rest of your life, it makes you feel even more hopeless, more in despair, and more worthless, and like, 'Why even try? Why even try? This pain is going to last forever.'"

These are clearly serious and sensitive matters—especially with the heightened suicide rate. But this is precisely why it feels so important to shine a light on more hopeful possibilities, which begins with recognizing other perspectives that cover up this hope. More than once, we've heard or witnessed stories of people reaching the point of active suicidality, at least in part, because they are convinced no future is possible where they can find real healing.

Lifelong Management—"I'll Always Need This To Be Okay."

Once someone is persuaded of both enduring brain impairment and lifelong emotional struggle, it's only natural to conclude that their need for outside intervention and ongoing support is also lifelong.

One woman told us about coming to accept a need for antidepressants that would never go away: "I'm just always gonna have to have something." A father told us about his daughter, "I don't think there's going to be a time that she's going to be well. We're going to have to stay on it, stay on it, stay on it forever."

When you reach this conclusion under the influence of a professional, it's pretty hard to question. "I was disposed to believe this doctor, that my brain was like a car engine that didn't have oil in it," said Thomas. "Which brings up this natural question; 'Where do I get oil? And how much does this oil cost? And where can I get a reliable supply, because the last thing I want is to break down.'"

No one would dispute the benefits that many have found from medical support—especially in the short-term. However, the evidence for benefit over the long-term is far less clear[10]—and deserves more attention in a time where long-term usage continues to increase. According to a 2019 *New York Times* analysis of federal data, more than 15 million Americans have taken antidepressants for at least five years—a rate that has more than tripled since 2000.[11]

This dramatic increase in long-term medication use has occurred despite concerning signals in the available research findings. A number of studies comparing medicated versus unmedicated depression have found that those taking medication long-term often have poorer outcomes. While this doesn't necessarily mean medication triggers worse outcomes (it could be that those with more severe depression are more likely to stay on medication), it does question a status quo that places more and more people on a pathway of indefinite medication usage.

Some people clearly do benefit from ongoing treatment and should be supported in getting whatever help they need. But that's not true of everyone. And regardless of how long treatment ought to continue, it could be helpful to appreciate how a narrative that insists people *must* take medications long-term can feel heavy to most.

After one of our presentations, we were approached by a woman who told us about a dear friend who had been grappling in recent years with some significant side effects from a psychiatric medication that was impacting her ability to be intimate with her husband. The doctor told her, "You'll need to be on these the rest of your life because your condition is lifelong." This woman went home, wrote a note to her husband and children, and ended her life.

We are certain this professional didn't intend to discourage this person's fragile heart, and he would have found the prospect that he did horrifying. As a rule, most doctors are very careful in how they speak so as to leave people encouraged and hopeful about their future. For patients already worried about the prospect of aching emotional pain continuing another week, this is just a reminder to be extra careful about channeling a message that undercuts any hope for longer-term healing. In this case, the idea of never being able to come off medication (for a condition that presumably would never go away) ended up being too much for this woman to handle.

Let's stop depressing those already depressed and discouraging those already discouraged. Thankfully, this is far from the only story we can tell.

A Hopeful Mental Health Paradigm Shift

To reiterate, if the available scientific research proved that mental and behavioral health problems were chronic conditions rooted in biological deficiencies, then we *should* help people accept that reality and whatever treatment is needed to cope.

However, as we will spell out in the next chapter—this simply isn't what the research is saying. There are literally tens of thousands of scientific studies converging around a hopeful paradigm that centers around the following:

1. **Environmental and lifestyle contributors:** There are a remarkably wide variety of contributing influences to conditions like depression, anxiety, and addiction.
2. **Biological changeability:** The changeability of the brain and the fluidity of genetic expression confirms how much hope people can have in the possibility of deeper, more sustainable healing from even severe mental health problems.
3. **Therapeutic lifestyle change:** Rather than attempting to merely control or manage symptoms, if you alleviate core risk factors through targeted adjustments, you can help people gradually move towards deeper, more vibrant emotional health.

Environmental and Lifestyle Contributors—"How I Live Impacts How I Feel."

Research on "social determinants of health" has exploded in recent years. Although biological predispositions still play a role, attention in many quarters is shifting away from probing for defects inside human beings to the many surrounding factors repeatedly shown to influence our hearts and minds.

Scientists from Clark University and the University of Washington have argued that "the growing number of depressed people can be attributed to a 'depressogenic society'"—reflecting a culture "giving birth" to depression like bacteria in a petri dish.[12]

As University of Kansas professor Stephen Ilardi puts it, "Our brains were never designed for the sedentary, indoor, sleep-deprived, socially isolated, fast food laden, screen addicted, frenetic pace of modern life."[13]

What might this look like in everyday life? Consider these common scenarios:

» **Digital overwhelm:** The average American spends over seven hours daily on screens, with constant notifications fragmenting attention and disrupting natural thought patterns. Many report anxiety spikes when separated from their devices—yet paradoxically feel worse after extended social media use.

» **Nutritional deficits:** The standard Western diet—high in processed foods, refined sugars, and inflammatory oils—has been linked to increased depression rates. Countries with traditional diets rich in omega-3 fatty acids, whole foods, and fermented products consistently show lower depression prevalence.

» **Movement deprivation:** Our ancestors walked an estimated 8 to 10 miles daily. Today, many of us sit for over 10 hours daily. This dramatic reduction in physical movement disrupts not just our metabolism but our mood regulation systems.

Studies consistently show that even modest increases in movement significantly reduce depressive symptoms.

- **Sleep disruption:** Before electric lighting, humans typically slept eight to nine hours nightly with patterns aligned to natural light cycles. Today's artificial lighting, screen exposure, and 24/7 schedules have dramatically altered our sleep architecture, with an estimated one-third of adults chronically sleep-deprived—a condition strongly correlated with depression and anxiety, and all sorts of other health problems.
- **Social disconnection:** Despite our hyperconnected world, meaningful face-to-face interaction has plummeted. Researchers at Harvard have tracked a steady decline in close confidants, with the average American reporting fewer intimate relationships than previous generations.[14] This social isolation creates conditions where depression flourishes.
- **Nature deficit:** Humans evolved in natural settings, yet most now spend 90 percent of their time indoors. Research shows that even brief nature exposure—a twenty-minute walk in a park—can reduce stress hormones and measurably improve mood.[15] Urban environments without green spaces also correlate with higher rates of mental health challenges.

Does any of this describe your own life? If so, do you think it could be influencing how you feel emotionally? The good news is that each of these factors represents not just a risk but an opportunity—a practical pathway toward feeling better that doesn't depend exclusively on medication or therapy (though these remain valuable tools for many).

Throughout this book, we'll explore simple, evidence-based adjustments to counter these "depressogenic" forces—changes that have helped thousands reconnect with emotional wellbeing even without dramatic life overhauls. Small shifts in how you eat, move, connect, and rest can profoundly impact how you feel—often within days and weeks, instead of having to wait months and years.

Biological Changeability—Fluid Genes, Changeable Brain

Even if it's true that many conditions around us impact our emotional health, some legitimately wonder, "Well, what does this matter if my body is still sick?" As one woman told us, "Exercise doesn't matter for me, because I have a chemical imbalance."

A second pillar of this alternative paradigm is new appreciation for how our body itself gets shaped by both pleasant and unpleasant experiences, which each imprint our brain in a way that impacts our emotional health, for better or worse.

And that's actually great news because the same brain that gets changed by difficult experiences can be shaped and rewired by positive ones too. Listen to these summaries from the experts:

- "The experiences we undergo, the choices we make, and the acts we undertake inscribe a diary on the living matter of our cortex. . . . The life we lead, in other words, leaves its mark in the form of enduring changes in the complex circuitry of the brain—footprints of the experiences we have and the actions we have taken. . . . It is the life we lead that creates the brain we have."—Dr. Jeffrey Schwartz, UCLA Department of Psychiatry[16]
- "The brain is . . . a talented learning machine. Nothing is completely fixed. Biology powerfully affects but does not lock in our reality."—Dr. Louann Brizendine[17]
- "The bottom line is the brain is wired to adapt. . . . There's no question that rewiring goes on all the time."—Steve Yantis, Neuroscientist, Johns Hopkins University

This understanding of neuroplasticity—the brain's ability to reorganize itself throughout life—represents one of the most profound scientific revolutions of our time. As recently as the 1990s, scientists believed the adult brain was largely fixed and unchangeable. Today, we know the brain remains remarkably adaptable throughout our lives. Every experience, thought pattern, and lifestyle choice literally reshapes our neural architecture.

What about our genes? Many of us were taught that genes are a static blueprint that gets laid down linearly in our lives. But Barbara McClintock won the Nobel Prize for demonstrating how genetic expression can change depending on how we live, in what she called the "fluid genome."

That means depending on our choices, we can turn on or off the expression of certain genes that play a role in our emotional and behavioral health. Isn't that exciting?

Therapeutic Lifestyle Change—Small Changes Are Not Small

If it's true that our brain and body can heal and grow over time and that the original source of so much emotional pain comes from outside of us, then it's *game on*. A whole new world of healing opens up. One centered around your own choices, relationships, and life as a whole.

Don't worry, this is not about having to change your whole life. Even small adjustments can make significant differences in your mood. As you will see in the next chapter, even *single* changes in *one* lifestyle area can generate a significant emotional boost. That boost grows even larger when we gain momentum and make changes in multiple areas.

Celebrating the Upward Spiral

We all know what a vicious cycle looks like—where one negative experience triggers another. This paradigm shift showcases a cycle in exactly the opposite direction—a momentum-generating positive cycle, where small life changes that help tune even one brain circuit "just a tiny bit" can spark other changes that have a surprising ripple-effect on our mood.

Earlier, we cited neuroscientist Alex Korb describing how physical activity can spark a positive rippling effect by shifting electrical activity in the brain during sleep, which can then reduce anxiety, improve mood, increase energy, etc. He emphasizes, "*Any tiny change* can be just the push your brain needs to start spiraling upward," before elaborating:

> Everything is interconnected. Gratitude improves sleep. Sleep reduces pain. Reduced pain improves your mood. Improved mood reduces anxiety, which improves focus and planning. Focus and planning help with decision making. Decision making further reduces anxiety and improves enjoyment. Enjoyment gives you more to be grateful for, which keeps that loop of the upward spiral going. Enjoyment also makes it more likely you'll exercise and be social, which, in turn, will make you happier.[18]

This interconnection means that improvement in one area often leads to unexpected benefits in others. For instance, people who begin a simple walking routine often report not just improved mood but better sleep, which can subsequently lead to better food choices, all of which provides more energy for meaningful activities. This cascade effect means you don't have to transform everything at once—you just need to find your best entry point into the upward spiral.

What positive momentum and upward spiral is waiting to take off in your life? And what's the first domino that needs to fall to get it moving?

Watching for Clues

Let's connect a few more dots before diving into the research more. In addition to pointing toward more hopeful trajectories, this paradigm shift also says something about the pain itself. Rather than a crisis to manage, emotional distress in this vantage point becomes a signal that something is wrong—a clue we can explore with Sherlock

Holmes's curiosity, looking for adjustments that might help. As best-selling author Johann Hari, with his own story of mental health recovery, summarizes:

> Your distress is not a malfunction. It is a signal—a necessary signal. I know this is going to be hard to hear, because I know how deep your suffering cuts. But this pain isn't your enemy, however much it hurts. This pain is your ally—leading you . . . and pointing the way toward a more fulfilling (life). You are at a fork in the road now. You can try to muffle the signal. That will lead you to many wasted years when the pain will persist. Or you can listen to the signal and let it guide you—away from the things that are hurting and draining you, and toward the things that will meet your true needs.[19]

Our work over the last decade has been developing tools to help people listen to these clues in their own lives and then learn about targeted lifestyle adjustments that can help them move in a new direction.

Renewed Hope

Please don't misunderstand. This alternative paradigm doesn't naively promise dramatic healing to everyone. For different reasons, some people suffer more than others—and for longer periods of time. But as we mentioned at the beginning, there's a big difference between some hope and no hope.

One woman told us about the moment when a doctor told her whole family, "She won't live independently the rest of her life." From a later interview *in her own apartment*, this woman spoke of "how much power that single statement had on everyone." Then she said, "Never predict the recovery of another person."

Don't do it. Not in either direction. Not, "You're going to get better soon!" And not, "This will probably be your life." Why? Because there are too many variables.

Let the future open—leaving the door open for something to surprise you in a good way. There is really good evidence that this kind of hope is not secondary when it comes to finding deeper healing. One of the foremost recovery researchers, Dr. Daniel Fisher, states, "The belief that one can recover from mental illness is well established as an important aspect of the healing experience"—noting from his own interviewing research with distressed individuals, "Over and over again, we heard, 'I needed someone to believe in me.'"[20]

"The important thing is that I know that it won't last forever," said one depression survivor. "Before, I had no hope. I couldn't see a light at the end of the tunnel." Another recovered person said, "Having some hope is crucial to recovery; none of us would keep trying if we believed it a futile effort."

Please stay hopeful! Encourage others around you to do the same—especially if they feel broken inside. As Jon Kabat-Zinn, contributing author of *The Mindful Way Through Depression*, said, "As long as you're breathing, there is more right than wrong with you—no matter what you are facing."[21]

"You have a well part in you, and it's a beautiful part. Never forget that," Dr. Daniel Dorman would tell his clients struggling emotionally. In an interview, he reiterated to us, "That person suffering is not to be underestimated. Growth and development are possible. There is no such thing as permanently stunted growth. The capacity to grow and develop is present in everyone."

Chapter 3

The Science Behind the New Paradigm

The evidence is in—and it's remarkably hopeful. Thousands of studies support a new understanding of emotional well-being that empowers rather than limits us. This chapter explores the scientific foundation of a more optimistic approach to mental health.

It's not hard to understand why people are so skeptical of scientific pronouncements these days. In the cultural and health conflicts of the last decade, too often science has been weaponized in an attempt to establish the dominance of one side (and shut down the other).

The greatest tragedy of this sort of activist science is that it closes down the beautiful potential that a collective practice of humble, sincere, high-quality investigation has to inform our pursuit of the full truth as a human family.

If we lay aside the culture war hostilities, widespread paranoia, and entrenched suspicion infecting so much of modern discourse, then what does the available high-quality research on mental health actually suggest?

Something *pretty darn sweet.*

Enormous Reasons for Hope

Especially when things feel dire, human beings rightly look to many transcendent sources for inspiration and encouragement—from poetry to scripture to art. What many don't realize is how much "boring ol' scientific literature" confirms some remarkable hope when it comes to healing and recovery from emotional and behavioral problems, including in regard to serious forms of depression, anxiety, and addiction.

Thanks to the hard work of a global community of investigators, there are a few empirical touchpoints that can help ground our intuitions and expectations for healing. This includes studies exploring:

1. **Neuroplasticity:** An explosion of over 72,300 scientific articles now document exciting possibilities surrounding the brain's ability to be malleable.
2. **Risk factors:** The science backs this up in a big way. Thousands of studies (over 88,000) have uncovered what can trigger depression and anxiety in our lives. Similar research (63,000 articles) reveals what sets us up for addiction. This isn't just theory—it's well-documented evidence that gives us a roadmap to recovery.
3. **Lifestyle adjustments:** Well over 100,000 scientific papers have explored the beneficial impact of lifestyle interventions (nutrition, exercise, sleep, stress) for those facing serious emotional and behavioral health challenges.
4. **Mindfulness practice:** Another 11,000 different scientific articles have investigated the health benefits of mindfulness and meditation, including for bolstering sobriety and healing from depression and anxiety.
5. **Behavior change:** Key mechanisms and processes associated with measurable change in behavioral patterns have likewise been examined in over 150,000 scientific articles.

To put these numbers in perspective, the entire medical research base examining the most widely prescribed antidepressants consists of fewer than 5,000 studies. The evidence base for lifestyle and environmental approaches to mental health is of a magnitude larger than what supports our current pharmaceutical-focused paradigm.

It seems important to highlight the large numbers of studies above, if only to illustrate the enormous research momentum in each of these areas. But, of course, numbers of studies alone don't tell us enough. It's what the collective body of researchers found that's the cause for real excitement.

Neuroplasticity

Before scientists discovered the degree to which even adult brains continue to change throughout the lifespan, it was widely assumed that a problem like serious mental illness involves brain patterns that were probably permanent.

Brain scientists don't believe this anymore—and *neither should you*. For the last twenty years, discovery after exciting discovery has confirmed the surprising malleability of the brain. This is true for old brains and young brains, male and female brains, and yes, sick and healthy brains. Even when brain injuries take place during car accidents, research has found that remarkable changes can take place in the physiology over time.[1]

The discovery of neurogenesis—the brain's ability to generate new neurons throughout life—was so revolutionary that scientists initially rejected it. Until the 1990s, the scientific consensus held that humans were born with all the brain cells they would ever have. We now know that certain brain regions, particularly the hippocampus (crucial for memory and emotion regulation), continue to produce new neurons well into our eighties and nineties.

For instance, even meditation alone has been shown to change the structure and function of the brain.[2] So does better sleep[3] and an improved diet.[4] What do these kinds of discoveries mean for people facing depression, anxiety, or addiction? Rather than simply coping with and managing an enduring brain deficiency, some fascinating innovators have been exploring a wide range of practical strategies that can help expedite brain changes associated with deeper and more lasting healing.

Bottom line: If you change your life in concrete ways (better food, better sleep, more physical activity, less stress, improved relationships, and increased spirituality), it will change your brain too . . . improving your mental and emotional health in many ways.

Risk Factors

While there have been many valuable scientific investigations into the experience of mental health and addiction, few realize how much rigorous study has also gone into the many different precursor environmental and lifestyle conditions that *set people up* for these same crippling problems (making it more or less likely that emotional or behavioral problems will show up in the first place).

The medical literature documents an array of risk factors that predispose both mental health struggles and compulsive-addictive patterns. In fact, it was our own review of these extensive literatures that first prompted our excitement at what this knowledge could mean practically for people suffering with paralyzing emotional or behavioral struggles—especially if they had some extra support to implement those adjustments in their lives.

What stands out the most is the breadth of potential contributors involved. What if people could catch this vision of wide-ranging factors potentially influencing them? How might it change their perception of their struggle and their likely futures?

Single Lifestyle Adjustments

It's not just lifestyle patterns setting people up for problems like depression or anxiety that have received scientific attention. There's also a surprising amount of evidence documenting what happens emotionally when specific adjustments to these same lifestyle and environmental factors take place.

We've been inspired by research studies that take a single domain of risk—such as physical inactivity, poor nutrition, or disrupted sleep—and implement one intervention designed to spark change in a better direction.

It's striking to witness measurable improvements that happen in emotional well-being associated with a *single change*. For instance, a 1999 study at Duke University Medical Center found that a brisk thirty-minute walk or jog around the track three times a week may be just as effective in relieving symptoms of major depression in the short-term as antidepressant medications.[5]

A later 2017 controlled study found that people who changed their diets (and nothing more) were significantly better compared to a control group—with approximately 30 percent no longer depressed (compared to 8 percent in the control group).[6]

Mindfulness meditation has also been shown in a 2004 study by researchers at UC Irvine and Oxford to cut depression relapse in half.[7] And a 2021 study in the *Journal of American Medical Association* jointly conducted by the University of Colorado at Boulder, MIT, and Harvard likewise demonstrated that going to bed one hour earlier and waking up one hour earlier—without any other change—can reduce the risk of depression by 23 percent.[8]

Multiple Lifestyle Adjustments

Given the impact of single lifestyle changes, we've been even more intrigued to see investigations of what happens when people change more than one of these factors at a time. So, what happens when people facing emotional struggles make adjustments in a number of areas? The results are remarkable.

In a study of 4200 people, Dr. Neil Nedley found that over 90 percent of people facing both depression and anxiety found some significant improvement after making lifestyle adjustments across a number of areas—with 85 percent having a response rate of at least 50 percent reduction in symptoms.[9]

Dr. Stephen Ilardi at Kansas University also observed clinically significant improvement in 77 percent of those who participated in the "therapeutic lifestyle change" program for depression—including many who failed to get better with other treatment approaches. These improvements were still going strong months later, with no significant relapse.[10]

As you can see, these are not short-term impacts. The same research team found that systematically improving lifestyle risk factors didn't just reduce depression and anxiety rates dramatically—participants also showed continuing improvement six months after the study was complete.[11]

This is all consistent with our own internal data reviews, which show a dose-response relationship among participants between key outcomes (sobriety, depression, and anxiety) and the degree to which they were willing to learn more and make life adjustments. The more intensive people's investment in learning and changing, the more their symptoms decrease.

We've seen that over and over—with incremental increases in lifestyle areas (at a 5 to 10 percent level) corresponding with emotional well-being improvements at double or triple the rate (20 to 35 percent increases).

Mindfulness Practice

One of the lifestyle adjustments that is receiving the most scientific attention is what happens when people infuse their experiences, especially painful ones, with more space, silence, and stillness. As people learn to approach a difficult problem from a gentler, calmer place, research consistently documents how that problem changes significantly for the better: less pain, more relief.

This isn't just a psychological effect, either—with the brain and body showing several changes when we practice bringing ourselves to a place of stillness and calm, over and over. White and gray matter change in the brain, genetic expression shifts, and the body gradually moves out of fight-and-flight mode in a way that reactivates our prefrontal cortex.

In everyday life, this might look like pausing to notice physical sensations of anxiety without judgment, creating space between an urge and action with addiction, or simply taking three conscious breaths before responding to a stressful situation. Research from institutions like Johns Hopkins shows that this "turning toward" difficult emotions (rather than our knee-jerk tendency to run or push away from them) can significantly reduce their intensity within minutes.[12]

The practice of mindfulness doesn't require hours of meditation.

Even brief moments of mindful awareness—while eating, walking, or during daily transitions—gradually build what neuroscientists call "response flexibility": the ability to choose our reactions rather than being driven by them.

All of that matters a lot for people facing serious emotional and behavioral struggles—which is why we've spent so many years at Impact Suite trying to create high-quality training and guidance about how exactly to take a more mindful approach to these struggles.[13]

Behavior Change

Over the last three decades, significant attention has gone to scientifically analyzing key mechanisms and processes involved in reaching lasting behavioral change. We've paid particular attention to the takeaway discoveries in creating our technological infrastructure and the specific content and strategies housed within.

Some of those key discoveries include:

» **Gamification as a catalyst to healing.** There are a growing number of scientific articles exploring ways that principles from gaming can help catalyze healing and change ("gamification").[14] In our own technological work, we've found ways in which this lighter-hearted, playful approach can help shift people out of a "fight-or-flight" mentality—into a more resilient, open place where deeper learning and growth can take place. Dr. Ben Sawyer at MIT describes "seductive, ubiquitous, lifelong health interfaces" as a great value for "well-being self-care."[15]

» **Digital interventions.** A total of 67,000 published articles examine the use of digital, mobile, and online platforms for both educational purposes and as a complement to medical and psychological services. One research team found the effectiveness of such interventions is enhanced when they are combined with an offline, not just virtual, social encounter.[16]

» **Awareness enhancement.** Even though we *should* be the expert of our own lives, there are so many things we miss. That helps explain why "self-monitoring is a core feature of many behavioral and psychological therapies and has been recommended as an important component in the delivery of digital mental health."[17] Digital health interventions have been emphasized as helpful to monitor changing signs of well-being. These are noted as potentially "extreme utility in sessions when clients could not remember how they've been feeling since their last session."[18]

» **Self-determination.** Consistent with the value of self-monitoring, self-guidance and direction is also of great interest to users—as one team called it, "self-participatory care."[19] Health interventions have been shown to be more effective when they "support self-management."[20]
» **Highlighting the positive.** In one study, participants expressed concern that "continuous [symptom] monitoring may become tiresome and could lead people to unhelpfully dwell on experiences." This underscores the importance of registering "positive events for people to identify, recognize, and acknowledge." A 2009 study of studies of positive psychology interventions that aim to cultivate positive feelings, behaviors and/or cognitions found they "enhance well-being and ameliorate depressive symptoms—especially when people are struggling emotionally.[21]
» **Giving people options.** One central finding in an in-depth review of internet-delivered interventions promoting health behavior change in 43,236 different participants was that "Interventions that incorporated more behavior change techniques tended to have larger effects than interventions that incorporated fewer techniques."[22] Dr. Joseph Grenney writes, "It is not the strategies in-and-of themselves that make the difference, it is how many of the strategies you choose to employ at one time. The more strategies, the more successful the odds of changing the behavior."[23]

What these findings reveal is a fundamental shift in how we understand the healing process—from a passive "being treated" model to an active "participating in healing" approach. This aligns with research on internal versus external locus of control, which consistently shows that people who believe they have agency in their recovery experience better outcomes than those who believe their health is entirely in the hands of external forces or experts.

Reaching More People

Based on these kinds of results, one researcher declared that the "scaling up" of efforts to encourage incremental lifestyle adjustments ought to be a "key imperative" in the future.[24] Dr. Roger Walsh of the University of California, Irvine's College of Medicine noted: "Lifestyle changes can offer significant therapeutic advantages for patients, therapists, and societies, yet are insufficiently appreciated, taught or utilized"—pointing out that these approaches were effective, inexpensive, and often enjoyable with few side effects and complications.[25]

That's why he called for "wide scale" lifestyle-oriented interventions, concluding, "Given the enormous mental, physical, social, and economic costs of contemporary lifestyles, such interventions may be essential. In the 21st century, therapeutic lifestyles may need to be a central focus of mental, medical, and public health."[26]

One of the most compelling aspects of this approach is its accessibility. While conventional treatments face significant barriers—cost, stigma, provider shortages, side effects—many lifestyle interventions can be implemented with minimal resources. A walking program costs nothing; mindfulness practices can be learned from free online resources; and nutritional improvements are often cost-neutral or even cost-saving compared with processed food.

The implications are profound: The most effective mental health interventions may also be the most accessible and sustainable. Once again, this doesn't mean medication and therapy aren't valuable—they certainly are for many people. Rather, it suggests that discussions about our first-line approaches should include these foundational lifestyle modifications—with more intensive interventions added when needed.

The science is clear: Hope for mental health recovery isn't just a comforting platitude—it's a robust, evidence-based position aligning with a stunning amount of data. The real question isn't whether improvement is possible; it's how we can best support everyone interested in learning how to tap into these encouraging pathways to healing.

Part II

What Can We Learn from Those Who Have Found Healing?

Chapter 4

Learning From Those Who Find Healing

Enormous attention goes to those facing agonizing emotional pain that doesn't seem to let up. However understandable this may be, we may be missing a lot when our focus (research, policy, news, public discourse) keeps getting absorbed in situations of more chronic struggle.

What if we paid more attention to people who have found healing as well? This has been a burning question for us ever since we learned about a remarkable researcher named Kelly Turner. Dr. Turner noticed something unusual in her early studies at the University of California at Berkeley. Very few questions were being asked about the over one thousand cases of "spontaneous" or "radical" remission from cancer, where someone heals in a statistically unlikely way after conventional medicine has failed. So she set about doing just that—conducting interviews and eventually gathering hundreds of stories from all around the world. [1]

Dr. Turner's findings are summarized in her bestseller, *Radical Remission: Surviving Cancer Against All Odds*, now translated into twenty-two languages—along with *Radical Hope: 10 Key Healing Factors from Exceptional Survivors of Cancer & Other Diseases*. Her work has been an inspiration to many families facing cancer and a reminder to the rest of us how often we can overlook lessons from those who have found lasting healing.

Dr. Turner's approach represents what scientists call "positive deviance research"—studying outliers who succeed against the odds in order to discover insights that might help others. This methodology has transformed practices in fields from malnutrition to hospital infections. Rather than analyzing what goes wrong, this approach asks, "Who is getting it right, and what can we learn from them?" The same question that sparked Dr. Turner's cancer research has guided our investigation into mental health recovery.

Fixated on the Hardest Realities

Those who have studied the history of psychology can appreciate how much the entire field could benefit from this kind of a reminder. Even those who love psychology know the field has had a fixation on lurid and worst-case scenarios for a long time. That's precisely why positive psychology efforts from Martin Seligman, Barbara Fredrickson, and many others have been so influential and so refreshing.[2]

Yet a fixation on the negative has a momentum of its own. "People don't get better from this," one doctor told us. So convinced are some about the impossibility of healing that when they hear a story of someone claiming to have experienced lasting emotional healing, their first inclination is to doubt that the person had ever experienced "real" mental illness or addiction in the first place.

This dismissive response to recovery stories reveals a powerful cognitive bias in mental health care. When patients don't recover, the prevailing narrative about chronic illness seems to be repeatedly confirmed. But when they do recover, instead of questioning that same dispiriting narrative, the diagnosis is often questioned—especially by medical practitioners and some mental health clinicians, but also sometimes by family and friends. This confused reasoning has prevented us from seriously studying recovery as a phenomenon worthy of scientific attention.

But they're missing something exciting! As we've pursued an approach similar to Dr. Turner, gathering long-term healing stories of depression, anxiety, and addiction over recent years, we've seen story after story that began in enormous pain—with conditions just as serious as other severe cases of depression, anxiety, and addiction. But that's not where these stories end.

We've gathered these stories of recovery from many places online—including YouTube and in published memoirs—as well as from people in our own networks who have been willing to share their stories with us. Documenting and curating these stories has been exciting, even exhilarating at times. With the same eagerness we used to collect basketball and baseball cards, we now collect stories of profound emotional healing. It's not uncommon for one of these stories to take our breath away in its beauty and power.

We believe there's an urgency to gathering these stories. It's common for people facing depression and anxiety to ask, "Has anyone ever overcome this?" And one woman facing compulsive-addictive patterns described how she would "go on YouTube and seek stories of people who had been delivered."

Whether or not that someone takes steps towards deeper, more lasting healing may well depend on whether they find a story of someone else that's done the same. Alternatively, that person may end up coping and just barely managing year after year.

Lessons and patterns across these diverse experiences of transformation are what we aim to document in the pages that follow.

The Variety of Stories Gathered

In the following chapters, we review what we've learned so far—outlining patterns and themes that keep showing up. This gathering of stories will continue as an ongoing project, and we anticipate more learning to come—with continued updates, which we anticipate sharing.

Naturally, the stories gathered vary a great deal. Some of the accounts are more autobiographical and centered primarily on direct experiences, while others are interwoven with life lessons and advice to other sufferers. Sometimes they are shorter and sometimes longer—with a full library of beautiful memoirs we've been able to enjoy.

This points to one of the central limitations of the project. Ideally, each and every person could have been interviewed personally in order for them to answer all the same questions. While we were able to conduct these kinds of interviews with some people, the rest were already published accounts that were gathered through a variety of other means.

Practically speaking, this means our knowledge is limited by what people chose to share or not share—with standardized, statistical assessments not possible in this dataset. For that reason, as a complement to this narrative analysis, we share below some statistical patterns from surveys of our own app users who come to us seeking lasting healing and freedom.

Living Different Lives

Over the last year, we've asked people at various stages of healing to share with us patterns they see in their own lifestyles. Although there are many interesting trends, the most significant finding could be summarized in this simple statement:

People who experience lasting healing from mental health challenges and addiction live differently than those who struggle to find the same kind of healing.

Is this because healing also naturally leads people to a different kind of life? At least in part, that must surely be the case. We've also seen enough evidence in our own analyses and other external studies to know that this influence runs both ways. Without question, people who make certain adjustments in their lives are also more likely, over time, to find deeper healing.

To illustrate this, we now provide two detailed comparisons: the first between people doing well or poorly in their struggle with depression and anxiety and the second between people finding freedom (or not) from compulsive-addictive struggles with pornography (the combined sample size is 250—large enough to detect meaningful patterns).

No matter where participants found themselves in their healing journey, we asked them to review a list of well-known lifestyle influences on deeper recovery. Each was asked to evaluate how much these influences showed up in their life today or in prior years.

Antidepressant Lifestyle Patterns

The first list below shares patterns from those who reported "experiencing deeper healing and relief from depression or anxiety for some time now" as compared with those who told us they are "struggling right now emotionally, and haven't ever really found much lasting relief from depression or anxiety."

The biggest gap is a 55 percentage point difference in reported stress management between groups—with 85% of people who have experienced significant emotional healing saying, "I manage my stress quite well," while only 30% of those who are still struggling with depression and anxiety say the same. In addition, we found the following differences (in order from largest to smallest):

Lifestyle Pattern	Percentage Reporting This Who Experience Healing	Percentage Reporting This Who Still Struggle	Percentage Point Difference
"I've been able to relate to thoughts and emotions more mindfully—and less personally and literally."	98%	50%	48
"I have found significant meaning and purpose in my life."	98%	50%	48
"I get pretty good sleep that leaves me mostly rested."	83%	40%	38

"I participate in spiritual practices like prayer, worship and scripture reading."	88%	50%	38
"I manage my time quite well."	83%	45%	38
"I've tapered back on a prescribed medication that was affecting my emotions." (Among those who were previously taking medication.)	73%	36%	37
"I've been able to talk about and make progress working through painful things from my past." (Among those who report prior trauma)	98%	66%	37
"I notice when I start ruminating (repetitive, anxious, or worrisome thoughts) and do my best to stop."	90%	58%	32
"I have experienced healing from compulsive patterns in my life (e.g., substance, media, spending)." (Among those who report previously struggling with compulsivity)	91%	59%	32
"I've become more connected in healthy ways to friends or family."	93%	65%	28
"I regularly eat healthy foods."	90%	65%	25
"I've learned many important lessons that have helped me heal."	98%	75%	23
"I've made a number of meaningful changes in my life."	98%	75%	23
"I'm physically active and exercise when I can."	85%	70%	15

"I manage my money quite well."	90%	75%	15
"I limit sugar, caffeine, and junk food."	74%	60%	14
"I prioritize time with family and friends who are important in my life."	98%	85%	13
"I've stayed hopeful about the possibility of deeper healing in my life."	98%	85%	13
"I pay attention to what kind of news and entertainment media I take into my mind."	95%	85%	10
"I regularly have a chance to get outside and get some direct sunlight."	83%	75%	8
"I limit media that makes me mad, sad or fearful."	98%	90%	8

Looking at these patterns, several themes stand out: Aside from sleep and time-management, the largest differences show up in the mental, emotional, and spiritual domain—including cognitive flexibility (mindful relationship to thoughts), meaning and purpose, spiritual practice, tapering psychotropic medication, trauma healing, anti-rumination, and overcoming compulsivity. These align with research on neuroplasticity and stress physiology, suggesting that the most powerful lifestyle factors may be those that directly impact how we relate to our own thoughts and emotions—which more immediately impacts how we interpret difficult experiences and, ultimately, how well our stress response system functions.

There were also minor differences between groups as to whether they have "reduced dependence on alcohol or other recreational substances" and whether they "regularly meditate, do yoga, or experience stillness and silence." As you can see, there are many ways that people who experience lasting healing from depression or anxiety live differently than those who do not.

Anti-Addiction Lifestyle Patterns

The next list shares patterns from those who reported "experiencing lasting healing and growing freedom for some time now" from compulsive pornography use as compared with those who told us they are "struggling right now still and haven't really found much lasting freedom yet." We've ordered them again in order of the largest gaps first:

Lifestyle Pattern	Percentage Reporting This Who Have Experienced Healing from Compulsive Pornography	Percentage Reporting This Who Still Struggle with Compulsive Pornography	Percentage Point Difference
"I have experienced healing from other compulsive patterns in my life (e.g., substance, media, spending)."	77%	30%	47
"I've learned many important lessons that have helped me heal."	98%	57%	41
"I've made a number of meaningful changes in my life."	96%	55%	41
"I've stayed hopeful about the possibility of deeper healing in my life."	100%	60%	40
"I've been able to relate to thoughts and emotions more mindfully, and less personally and literally."	83%	45%	38
"I notice when I start ruminating (repetitive, anxious, or worrisome thoughts) and do my best to stop."	85%	49%	36

"I have found significant meaning and purpose in my life."	89%	53%	36
"I manage my stress quite well."	85%	49%	36
"I've become more connected in healthy ways to friends or family."	89%	55%	34
"I manage my time quite well."	83%	49%	34
"I pay attention to what kind of news and entertainment media I take into my mind."	96%	66%	30
"I get pretty good sleep that leaves me mostly rested."	72%	43%	29
"I've been able to talk about and make progress working through painful things from my past."	79%	51%	28
"I participate in spiritual practices like prayer, worship and scripture reading."	90%	66%	24
"I regularly eat healthy foods."	87%	66%	21
"I regularly meditate, do yoga or experience stillness and silence in other ways (like art) to help my mind rest."	47%	30%	17
"I've tapered back on antidepressants, anti-anxiety drugs or other prescribed medication that was affecting my emotions."	15%	2%	13
"I manage my money quite well."	85%	73%	12

"I limit media that makes me mad, sad or fearful."	89%	77%	12
"I've reduced dependence on alcohol or other recreational substances."	43%	34%	10
"I regularly have a chance to get outside and get some direct sunlight."	85%	77%	8
"I'm physically active and exercise when I can."	79%	72%	7

When people overcome addiction to one thing (like pornography or alcohol), they often find it easier to break free from other bad habits, too. It's like learning to ride a bike—once you know how to balance on one bike, you can use those same skills on different bikes.

Our data shows that people who successfully recovered were much more likely to learn important lessons from their experience (98 percent compared to only 57 percent of those still struggling). This suggests that real recovery isn't just about stopping a behavior—it's also about changing how we think about ourselves and life overall.

This matches what scientists have found: People who stay addiction-free long-term usually develop new ways of understanding themselves and their place in the world. They don't just change what they do—they change how they see the world, including who they believe they are.

A more minor difference was found in those who say, "I limit sugar, caffeine and junk food." Once again, you can see that in many ways people who experience lasting freedom live differently than those who do not.

Learning from Healing Stories

No analytic approach we've taken—above or in subsequent chapters—proves causality nor is that our primary interest, since we presume a bidirectional relationship between all these variables. In other words, we take for granted that getting more or less physical activity influences mental health, which, in turn, naturally influences physical activity.

This still won't likely be definitive enough to persuade those who strongly doubt any prospect of lasting healing from serious mental illness. Yet combined with the other research reviewed in chapter three on lifestyle influences, we hope this at least sparks new discussions and greater openness to the possibility.

Others have been studying recovery stories for decades, including a well-known long-term project following the stories of people facing schizophrenia.[3] In line with our own findings detailed here, a 2011 review of nearly 100 articles on recovery narratives identified a set of common patterns showing up across stories, including: connectedness; hope and optimism about the future; identity; meaning in life; and empowerment—as well as a greater emphasis on spirituality and overcoming racial and mental illness–related stigma among individuals of Black and minority ethnic origin.[4]

Our specific aim in the coming chapters is to illustrate through people's own voices and experiences what the pathway of deeper, more lasting, and sustainable healing looks like for them in real-life color and detail.

Yet by definition, our attempt will be inescapably incomplete. Each of our participants has a profoundly rich experience that even a biography-sized volume wouldn't quite capture. And given the limitations in our access to that full experience, we're drawing conclusions based on those details that made it into their published stories.

What makes these real-life stories so valuable is that they show us how healing happens in the messy real world, not just in perfectly controlled lab studies. While scientific studies that carefully control variables (like randomized trials) are important, they often miss the complicated reality of people's actual lives. These personal stories keep all that real-life complexity intact, showing us how people actually heal while dealing with all of life's other challenges.

That, again, is why we're not presenting this report as final and definitive. Rather, it's a snapshot of what we've been able to review and learn so far—with more anticipated insight as we continue to gather more stories. As of this publishing, we have a number of additional stories to add to this growing analysis. (Please send other relevant stories our way at info@impactsuite.com.)

We hope that the following chapters will be encouraging to anyone grappling personally with the heavy weight of mental health and addiction—and to those who love them.

Chapter 5

Patterns in Lasting Healing from Mental Health Problems

When we study recovery stories closely, certain themes emerge again and again. These aren't just coincidences—they're valuable clues to what truly supports lasting healing.

On a personal level, most of us know how relieving it is to see a loved one begin to feel the emotional weight lifted after suffering for a period of time. We've watched our own family members and friends seeking that kind of relief, and sometimes finding it too.

Whenever we hear a story of someone finding relief from their emotional struggles, we're genuinely grateful to see that happen *and* we always wonder what will happen next. That's because we've studied these trajectories of healing long enough to know that we have to look over time to find out whether healing is really happening.

However familiar we've all become with poignant stories of serious depression and anxiety, and occasional relief that people find, what's far less familiar is what it actually looks like when people facing these kinds of intense emotional struggles find real healing that lasts.

The experiences related in this chapter are drawn from accounts of people who initially described overwhelming emotional pain. These stories were gathered through published memoirs, online YouTube accounts and other public writing, as well as our own interviews.

What unites them all—and became our "inclusion criterion" for the study—was that the story didn't end in continuing emotional pain. People whose accounts are gathered here all experienced healing to the point of being able to say something like, "For the first time in my life, I felt settled, calm and peaceful," or, "I had no idea I could ever be that happy."

Something special had clearly taken place in these stories. Mendek Rubin, a Holocaust survivor and author, describes a "seemingly endless sea of pain, fear, rage, guilt, grief and loneliness," which later became a "life of deep peace and boundless joy."[1]

Although these people still had challenging days, they were clearly in a different place than before. As one person said, "Now, when the rain comes, it rains, but it doesn't stay long enough to immerse and drown me."

These transformations weren't magical or instantaneous. They were gradual processes that unfolded through consistent attention to specific areas of life. While each person's journey was unique, clear patterns emerged across hundreds of stories—patterns that offer a roadmap for others seeking similar healing.

So how exactly do people arrive at this new place of emotional well-being? After listening to, reading, and reviewing hundreds of stories over the past decade, we've identified ten key themes that show up frequently across many stories of lasting recovery.

1. **Regaining confidence:** Restoring hope and taking ownership of the path to wellness.
2. **Seeking new understanding:** Gaining fresh perspectives on suffering and personal growth.
3. **Nourishing the body:** Strengthening your brain through nutrition, exercise, and sleep.

4. **Nourishing the mind:** Strengthening the mind through healthy input, exercise, and rest.
5. **Crafting supportive environments:** Designing spaces and routines that foster mental health.
6. **Practicing mindful awareness:** Approaching thoughts and emotions with gentle, nonjudgmental attention.
7. **Nurturing connections:** Building deeper relationships and strengthening emotional support networks.
8. **Healing past wounds:** Embracing forgiveness and working through traumatic experiences.
9. **Discovering purpose:** Expanding your sense of meaning, identity, and connection to others.
10. **Expanding emotional autonomy:** Increasing personal freedom and reducing long-term dependencies.

Many of these same themes show up prominently in the broader research literature touched on in chapter 3, as well as our own quantitative reviews in chapter 5. Think of these not as sequential steps but as interconnected elements that together create a foundation for healing. Let's explore how each of these elements contributes to lasting mental health recovery.[2]

1. Regaining confidence: Restoring hope and taking ownership of the path to wellness.

Hope is not incidental or secondary when it comes to lasting healing. "A sense of a positive future protects you," author Johann Hari says in his memoir. "If life is bad today, you can think—this hurts, but it won't hurt forever."[3] Across accounts, we found a number of people sharing things like, "I didn't want to just cope. I needed to hope that tomorrow could somehow be different."

Yet there were times when many felt otherwise: "Hopelessness was a huge part of my life for a very long time." Many recount hearing a professional say things like, "You will have to live with this for the rest of your life." Or, "Your clinical depression is a lifelong condition; your brain chemistry is permanently out of balance."

About a deeply painful time, Mendek recalls, "I was able to perceive the bare whisper of my inner voice telling me, 'Life is worth fighting for, no matter the price.' Otherwise, I would have perished."

"I had spent an entire lifetime believing I was at the whim of forces out of my control," writes Melissa Bernstein, founder of the toy company, Melissa & Doug.[4] She then describes "wallowing in negativity" and "drowning in futility over trying so desperately to control the uncontrollable, but no closer to doing so than I had ever been."

Eventually, Melissa felt a "small spark of possibility" that helped her begin "taking positive action each day" and which later contributed to "a sense of hope for the future."

This inner flicker of hope—sometimes barely perceptible—was often what people clung to during their darkest moments.

Ownership and responsibility.

Alongside hope, a surprising number of people describe arriving at a place where they realize greater power to direct their own healing process.

"If we believe we are ill because we have a problem that is beyond our own control," says one man, "then you simply set yourself up to be at the mercy of a force that cannot be held accountable for our actions."

Ashley highlights the personal impact of realizing "not that having a disease is a choice, but the way you approach your disease is a matter of choice, and that gives you back some element of power in your life." She adds, "That's incredibly important because the powerlessness pushes you under."

Athlete Alexi Pappas has spoken extensively in recent years about the impact of seeing her depression as an injury that could heal like any other: "I suddenly felt empowered," she has said, describing how this realization has helped her feel less helpless and more in control as she pursues deeper emotional healing.[5]

Healing reflection: Do you feel like you're in the driver's seat regarding your own healing journey? How encouraged do you feel at the prospect of additional healing ahead of you? What could you do to regain or expand that hope as a positive influence in your life?

Anti-addiction lifestyle challenge: Decide to own this journey of healing for yourself, appreciating how each moment and step in this adventure relies on your input. Say, "Exercising hope in the future is like a muscle—a future you take responsibility for pursuing, moment by moment." Write down on a sticky note one thing you'll say to yourself every morning for the next two weeks that encourages looking forward with more hope than before.

2. Seeking new understanding: Gaining fresh perspectives on suffering and personal growth.

Many describe some kind of learning that made a significant difference—picking up a book, watching a video, hearing a story, or meeting someone impactful.

> "I journeyed into an obscure bookstore and found books that taught me how to look inwards for more answers."
>
> "I looked at everything in my life under a microscope."
>
> "Gaining a fresh view about myself, others, and the world greatly impacted my healing."

This curiosity and hunger for understanding appears repeatedly in recovery stories. It stands in contrast to a narrowing of perspective that often accompanies depression and anxiety. The people who healed weren't passively waiting for solutions; they were actively seeking new frameworks to make sense of their experiences.

Look for clues behind the pain.

This process often reveals hidden patterns and influences previously unnoticed.

As one person shares, "determining factors of depression are often little things we are not aware of."

Thomas recalls thinking, "I'm exhausted; it's not working. I need to throw on the brakes and take account of what's going on." He continues, "When I did that for the first time, I was just really stunned by what I saw. My life was in total shambles."

Another says, "I came to realize that I had additional hurts, habits, and hang-ups to deal with in my heart," comparing the internal debris to the "dirt, filth, and junk piling up for years" in a neglected home.

Yet some point out this evaluation needs to be done gently. "We may not be in the place that we want to be," Vicki says, "but can we take a step back and thoroughly understand where we are?"

Johann says, "I've come to 'listen' to pain, rather than trying to muffle or silence or pathologize that pain." He continues, "Your distress is not a malfunction. It is a signal—a necessary signal . . . let it guide you—away from the things that are hurting and draining you, and toward the things that will meet your true needs."

Re-narrating the problem.

A number of people describe a burst of new hope as they come to see mental health problems in new ways:

"I had a beautiful, powerful a-ha moment" reading journalist Bob Whitaker's book *Anatomy of an Epidemic* about the mental health epidemic and "saw life in an entirely different way."

> "None of the realizations I've come to would have happened had I not been at least slightly open to thinking about things in a different way."

People also describe the power of reframing their struggles.

> "We have been systematically misinformed about what depression and anxiety are," Johann says. He describes the story that mental illness was "some kind of malfunction in the brain" as something that "made sense to [him]. It guided [him] through life," so much so that he felt hesitant to meddle with it. "I feared that if I messed with the story . . . the pain would be like an unchained animal, and would savage me." That didn't stop Johann from eventually embracing another view of depression more focused on the conditions of his life.

You are the author of your story. You get to stop and turn around or keep going at any point in your journey. You get to appreciate the everyday beauty in the simplest of things.

Healing reflection: How often have you learned new things about or from your emotional pain? What was the last thing you learned from the challenges you face? Where might you seek out more of this kind of insight?

Antidepressant lifestyle challenge: Don't stop learning. Consider each new insight and expanded perspective as a deepening of your healing. This week, commit to watching an interesting online presentation, reading a book that has made an impact in others' lives, or signing up for a program that someone you respect has found helpful.

3. Nourishing the body: Strengthening your brain through nutrition, exercise, and sleep.

Nutrition, physical activity, and sleep are widely embraced as crucial for physical health, yet some still scratch their heads as to why they matter for emotional health.

> Michael recalls, "I asked the psychiatrist whether he thought there was any link between nutrition and mental health. He looked at me as though I had just asked whether there was any link between mental health and UFO rectal probes."

Today, it seems that more people are appreciating the food-mood connection.

> Juanita describes being among those who were "sleep-deprived, ate too many fast-food meals, and dependent on caffeinated drinks"—eventually realizing the "many ways that [she] abused [her] body, mind, and spirit."

The brain-body connection is, of course, supported by thousands of research studies showing how inflammation, nutrient deficiencies, circadian rhythm disruption, and sedentary behavior directly affect mood and cognitive function. In the stories we analyzed, physical well-being wasn't just a nice bonus—it was often foundational and catalyzing for other kinds of healing.

Good mood food.

New foods and supplements are often emphasized in healing accounts.

> David describes how he "increased the amount of green vegetables" he was eating.
>
> William reports taking a new set of B vitamins "on the recommendation of my psychiatrist."
>
> Another person found she was "severely deficient in vitamin D," so she takes megadoses now—with a variety of benefits highlighted.

> "Once I started mainly eating fruits, vegetables, and healthy fats, eliminated white flour, and most meat, I noticed a difference in how I felt," another shares.

For many, this process involves trying different things and following hunches until something makes a difference.

> One person recalled, "Once the caffeine effect wore off, after a few hours, I would experience a hard emotional landing" and felt "more susceptible to negative mood swings."
>
> After a difficult emotional period, Michael was challenged by a doctor to stop consuming refined sugar, alcohol, and coffee. "Forget it," he thought. "What else do you have for me, because that's not going to happen." He eventually decided to accept a yearlong challenge. Although difficult at first, Michael describes one morning when "the haze in my mind had lifted. It was a clear, crisp, brilliant sunny day in my mind—the first such day of sunny internal weather for years."
>
> "What came out of my year without sugar, coffee, or alcohol?" he asks. "I got my life back. Whereas before I was a mess, with moods all over the place and energy levels in the gutter, for the past four years, I have felt energized and in control of my life."

Upping physical activity.

Gentle physical activity, like yoga or hiking, is highlighted in different stories as helpful. Others describe benefits from a more "vigorous exercise regimen."

> "I have found that running works the best for me to get the strongest antidepressant effects."
>
> Running with her dog taught one woman that "[you can] endure more than you think, and that there's no other depression therapy quite like pavement beneath your feet."

More light and "vitamin N" (nature).

From light therapy lamps to schedule adjustments, people describe a boost from increasing their exposure to light.

William describes "stand[ing] in the window of my apartment for a few minutes. During fall or winter, when sunlight is sparse, I use a light box."

"Being in nature is like an elixir. It's like drinking in health. I need it. All seasons."

"Going for a walk on the beach, or looking closely at a tree or a flower, always helps me return to peace."

Melissa Bernstein describes the impact of "being simply an observer" inside a "boundless ecosystem" outside. She reflects on being "aware of just how much was occurring without my involvement" in the natural world and how this helped "the clamor" in her head to "subside."[6]

Better sleep.

"I'm very sensitive to sleep deprivation," Vicki says. "So, I always try to get as much sleep as I can."

Diana describes the impact of "resting quietly even if I can't sleep," which helps provide her "adequate rejuvenation" for the day.

Thomas reports only later realizing how important this was: "It was in hindsight that I realized how significant sleep was in holding all my physical and mental health together."

Kyle says, "If I go without sleep and start partying a lot and get overextended and stressed, that's the recipe for madness for me." He continues, "You've gotta kinda watch this and not think that you can go without sleep just because it feels like you could. You can't do that to your brain for years on end. You've got to take care of your body because your body takes care of your brain."

Healing reflection: How well are you currently taking care of your body? Which of the "big 3"—nutrition, physical activity, and sleep—could you make some meaningful improvements in?

Antidepressant lifestyle challenge: Experiment with one adjustment this week to boost your physical health. Choose something sustainable that addresses your specific needs: drink at least three liters of water daily, spend fifteen minutes outdoors each day regardless of weather, or set a "bedtime preparation" alarm one hour before you should sleep. After two weeks, assess how this change affects your mood and energy.

4. Nourishing the mind: Strengthening the mind through healthy input, exercise, and rest.

Compared with wide attention to physical diet, exercise, and quality rest, far less public attention has gone to mental diet, mental exercise, and mental rest.

> As Thomas says, "We're all pretty sensitive to how we feel after a meal. I don't think we have the same sensitivity for what goes on with the mind."

Just as we wouldn't expect our bodies to thrive on a diet of junk food, our minds cannot flourish on a steady diet of negative, chaotic, or inflammatory input. The concept of "mental nutrition" emerged as a powerful theme in recovery stories—with many people becoming increasingly selective about what information, media, and conversations they allowed into their awareness.

Refining mental content.

After realizing his typical mental content felt like "sludge" emotionally, Thomas decided to become "more choosy" about what he consumed. He reports, "My relationships changed, and my relationship with literature changed, and the way I interacted with media, internet, things like that changed a lot."

Others echo this discovery:

> "I've found that steering clear of the anger and acrimony so abundant on the internet helps avoid a negativity that can trigger a depressive mood."
>
> "I feel less anxiety and depression since I stopped checking social media as often."

In addition to paring back negative and dark content, people describe upping the positive:

> "I listened to a lot of podcasts and read a lot of books, [which helped to] put me in a positive frame of mind."

Enhancing mental activity.

Julie says, "I'm quilting again regularly."

Others describe emotional lift from taking a class or diving into family history.

Another person describes the benefit of keeping hands and mind busy by coloring, reading novels, and listening to audiobooks—all of which helped shift her mind away from "racing and ruminating."

Prioritizing mental rest.

In addition to mental intake and activity, mental rest seems equally valuable:

> "I just stopped, and just sat still, and I just closed my eyes. I wasn't looking for anything in particular. My focus was not taking more *stuff* in, not seeking more stimulation—but to just really be in my own experience."
>
> "I found that a slow, warm, and quiet breakfast is the single most influential factor on how I will feel throughout the day. To this day, I get up early enough to not have to rush in the morning. . . . I don't check my phone or emails during this time. I

take the time to appreciate the food, the quietude, not allowing myself to think about any problems. I am simply present in the moment."

"It was in the moments I'd close my eyes, and tune out the noise to relax that I'd finally sense something different about myself. I started to change; I started to grow."

At the time he paused like this, Thomas recalls his life feeling like a "total disaster. . . . I was as broken and beat up as I felt, emotionally." And yet, in that moment of resting in a place beneath thoughts and feelings, he "observed this deep stillness, this profound calm."

Juanita initially felt disconcerted that her period of depression struggle was "filled with deep silence." Eventually she discovered that "silence too is a significant gift," since "marinating in the silence" helped her "break down the tough issues in [her] heart."

Being present.

This kind of raw presence was different from the more typical living-in-my-head normal experience for many.

As Mendek recalls, "Constant engagement with my thoughts prevented me from experiencing full contact with life. I couldn't enjoy the sweetness, security, and spontaneity that come with being truly united with the world around me."

Thomas likewise observes from his experience, "Overthinking our problems can become a form of resistance to the problem itself. Whatever your primary problem was, that is now side-lined, and what's taking up the majority of your moment-to-moment experience is a lot of thinking itself. We put up a barrier and are no longer engaged with what was initially painful and causing the problem."

Slowing down to relish small joys.

Robert speaks of having "regained the experience of small pleasures."

Mark finds "packets of joy in experiences large and small, obvious and hidden"—saying, "tucked away in every day are reasons

> to rejoice in being alive," but sometimes you have to "pull the blinders of depression off to see it." He describes storing up and treasuring "little notes, cards, letters, and photographs that come," which he calls his "memorabilia against depression."

Mendek relates how he treasures "every moment" with his young grandson, saying, "I stay present as we crawl through his plastic toy tunnel, dig holes in the sand, and even when he cries inconsolably." This reflected a broader life practice for him:

> I try to do only one thing at a time and appreciate everything—a child's laughter, the texture of a rose petal, clouds floating across the moon in the night sky. I pay attention from the moment I open my eyes in the morning and gaze out of my window at the beautiful mountains.

When sorrow threatens to overwhelm him, Mendek describes being able to relish the sweetness of "little, everyday moments of my life"—"a state of grace" in which he welcomes each day as "a glorious adventure." He says, "presence is where peace lives."

Healing reflection: How well do you take care of your own mind—starting with the mental content you take in on a regular basis through books and other various media sources? And how often do you allow your mind to rest and be still?

Antidepressant lifestyle challenge: Look for ways to improve your mental diet, or detox elements that bring you down. Consider going on a seven-day social media detox. Keep track of how many times you went to check social media and intentionally plan some moments of mental rest where you don't have to take anything into your mind.

5. Crafting supportive environments: Designing spaces and routines that foster mental health.

Details of people's day-to-day lived environment made a difference.

> Marsha says, "I learned the value of beauty, and that the effort to bring beauty into any setting is worth the work it entails."
>
> Another woman struggled to do the same; "always a generally neat and tidy person," Wendy was shocked by how her home "fell into disarray." She describes how impossible it felt at first to find any order: "Everything was totally overwhelming. Looking at my massive to-do list made me want to give up right away."

Our physical surroundings shape our mental states in profound ways. Research in environmental psychology confirms that cluttered, chaotic spaces increase stress hormones and deplete cognitive resources. The stories we collected revealed how seemingly small environmental changes—organizing a single room, creating a peaceful morning routine, or establishing boundaries around stressful obligations—often created ripple effects of improvement.

> "I needed to break things down into smaller chunks, one room at a time," Wendy recalls, adding, "Getting my kitchen organized was one of the best things I've ever done for myself and my family. I was happier, and I just felt lighter." This prompted her to become a professional organizer, encouraging others to ask, "If you could have just one room in your house organized, which one would make you feel happiest or the most relieved?"

De-stressing your life.

Other stories describe realizing the negative emotional impact of the amount of stress allowed.

> Juanita emphasizes the impact of "living an unbalanced life." She continues, "Every person or organization I was associated with wanted something from me. I had not yet developed the ability to set boundaries or have realistic expectations for myself."

"As I got older, I had no idea what a healthy relationship with money should be." Wendy says. "I didn't know how to create a budget or how to manage debt. Taking charge of our finances was one of the best things we did. It gave us so much freedom."

Being okay with hard things.

When it comes to different inescapable stressors, Marsha underscores the value of growing in "distress tolerance" and "emotion regulation."

Another person says, "Pain and difficulty *are* going to happen to you. Trying to fight this truth is pointless. I'm not suggesting a pessimistic, fatalistic attitude. You can passionately work hard to improve your life and still accept that your life will inevitably include difficulties."

Such acceptance can feel liberating, especially when inner resistance starts to lighten.

As Thomas puts it, "When you stop resisting, when you stop avoiding, and you *look*—you open your closet and look at that bogeyman, and you realize that you're *equal* to that task, and that you *can* look at it and it won't destroy you. It's a willingness to hold your life—*all* of your life—in awareness."

Healing reflection: What's your emotional atmosphere like at home, school, or work? What kinds of adjustments to your physical atmosphere or daily schedule could make that atmosphere more encouraging, reassuring, and inspiring? When stress or discomfort arise around you, how well are you able to sit with it patiently?

> **Antidepressant lifestyle challenge:** Identify and establish a "keystone habit" that can anchor your day and create positive ripple effects. This might be a morning ritual that includes no screens for the first hour, a midday pause for five minutes of deep breathing, or an evening practice of writing down three moments of peace you experienced. Choose something that resonates with you and commit to it for at least two weeks.

6. Practicing mindful awareness: Approaching thoughts and emotions with gentle, non-judgmental attention.

Many people describe struggling to know how to better navigate dark thoughts.

> Thomas describes his early experience: "Thoughts in and of themselves are fine—they're innocuous, they're just thoughts, but when all you have is thoughts," and "your whole experience is characterized by [an] unbroken stream of thoughts, they beat in on you."

This shift in relationship to thoughts—from being consumed by them to observing them with more space—represents one of the most powerful transformations in recovery stories.

Getting out of our heads.

Some eventually realize that their earlier responses to distressing thoughts weren't working. "My head was nothing more than a prison," Melissa says, "a direct channel to despair" as "I exhausted and depressed myself with crazy anticipations."

Others report:

"Thinking about how you feel will not help you feel better."

"Thoughts couldn't possibly solve the problems that stood in the way of my happiness."

"My husband is not a gamer, but we found that when he was ruminating, an hour session of games that occupied his mind 100% did wonders for stopping rumination."

Melissa notes, "Whenever I stopped thinking and turned angst into spontaneous action and positive creation, I felt exhilarated and at peace."

Pushing back on thoughts.

While many "believe you are your feelings and thoughts," Jonathan explains that he learned to see it differently.

Mendek describes learning "how dysfunctional it was to consider his beliefs to be facts," saying, "My thoughts were not my own, and often told me lies, but still I did their bidding." He adds that he often "felt trapped by [his] beliefs like an animal in a cage."

Thomas acknowledges that it takes a "lot of practice learning to just push back from the thought process, rather than getting absorbed [in mental content]" and assuming it is important and needs further interpretation, "which, of course, only leads to more thinking."

Observing thoughts as a practice.

Thomas goes on to reflect, "Just how calming it is to be *aware* of thought, as opposed to *being* thought." He explains further, "*Being* thought can be like being on a bucking bronco, right? And we're getting tossed all over the place. It's a lot nicer to be in the bullpen, behind those cages where the bull is bucking that poor cowboy around and say, 'Wow, I'd hate to be that guy right now.'"

What's amazing about becoming aware of thoughts, he says, is that "you certainly get better at it over time" and "there's an incentive built into the process, it feels *so good* to be able to take a break, take a little vacation from thought."

Training the mind.

What was previously experienced as a kind of "torture, being enslaved by the thought process," changes in one man's experience after learning to "push back" from the mental content and "just notice it."

By "no longer believing" any passing thought, Thomas was no longer controlled by "their doom and gloom"—describing how he now approaches difficult thoughts and feelings like "black clouds that pass by in the sky," letting them "drift by, even if it's slowly, like leaves on the river."

"Healing from depression starts in *your mind*," one woman says—before clarifying that the battle centers less on fighting and more on learning to "train your mind." She would ask herself, "Does this thought benefit my soul?" If the answer was no, she continues, "I immediately dropped that thought. Immediately. No sitting around and thinking about it." She adds, "I used to spend a lot of time reliving painful memories and wallowing in my hurt . . . What if I had done this instead? What if that had happened instead? All these thoughts had to go."

Robert describes "speaking the truth to depression's lies" and working to "eliminate negative thought patterns."

George says, "It is our thinking that betrays us."

Externalizing despairing thoughts.

Aaron concludes that toxic thoughts were "not coming from me."

Likewise approaching depression as a "separate entity" from his own mind, William speaks of "earmarking certain thoughts" as coming from his true self (e.g., *I want to get better*), compared with those coming from depression (e.g., *I'm worthless*)—a differentiation process that helps him "consciously and purposefully ignore" when "it's the depression talking."

Skillfully navigating the mindweather of emotions.

Like painful thoughts, difficult emotions are often something we push away and avoid. Juanita describes "years of anger stuffed and turned inward, ignored, or swept under the rug for the sake of politeness." She continues, "My anger went underground."

> I didn't take the time to process the pain. In fact, I had never allowed myself to grieve any of the losses I'd experienced, whether deaths, business setbacks, failures, broken relationships, or other disappointments. My way of coping with pain was to stuff it and keep moving.

She goes on to speak about learning "how to be with [her] feelings," which "seemed so foreign" to her at first. She continues, "Marinating in silence for all those many months was exposing emotions I had stuffed away for far too long."

Modern neuroscience confirms that mindfulness practices strengthen connections between the prefrontal cortex and the amygdala, allowing for greater emotional regulation even during difficult experiences.

Getting it out.

Out of a past with limited space for expression, Melissa reflects on how "this tangled mass of emotion had nowhere to go but into more darkness, pushing me even further within myself."

"When you hold everything inside, it's like closing the Ziploc bag on your feelings and letting the bad things grow," Crystal says. "The longer it sits, the grosser it will be, and the harder it will be to clean. So, we need to 'open' our hearts and get some airflow."

Another person says, "In order to stay healthy, I have to feel all my feelings instead of numbing myself to them."

Still others describe painting, the "therapeutic release of art," "playing piano," and "acting" as being helpful, providing what Ashley calls an "opportunity to sort through some chaos in a creative way."

Melissa similarly finds that "creating had become [her] pathway out of despair."

Resisting the depressive pull.

"I was quite surprised to recognize and learn that I had to resist a certain psychological seductiveness to depression," Mark says. "Who would have thought depression could be seductive?! Like a drug, it promised escape from life and all its struggle. All I needed to do was surrender to it, let it take over, and indulge in its permission to retreat and disappear from life."

Learning to respond to emotion skillfully.

"Our culture tells us to indulge our whims and emotions," another individual says. "Most people are completely at the mercy of their emotions—which are fickle and cannot be trusted. Emotions are unstable and can swing drastically from moment to moment. A life based on emotion is a life built on shifting sands."

By contrast, Thomas observes from his experience: "The awareness, the willingness to be present with an emotion, actually softens it, gives it a kind of permission to activate and do whatever it wants to do—whether it's anger showing up in the body, whether it's sadness showing up in the body. Our only other option is to deny it permission and push it down into the cellar where we keep all those unwanted emotions. I mean, if we don't *face* these things, if we don't make room for them, do we really think it goes away?"

He then describes how he has learned to work with challenging emotion: "I've just found this practice of letting emotional activity well up, and expand, and grow, and just show up in me in whatever way it wants to, to be so empowering. Because every time, if I'm willing to stick with the movement quality of the emotion, then eventually, at some point, like all things, it exhausts itself, it burns out, and we can ride those waves."

Welcoming the full spectrum of emotion.

Thomas continues, "As individuals, we usually have preferences in terms of what emotions are okay, or what's welcome. And it's often a negative emotion that we have such a problem with, like we're judgmental with ourselves for being angry, or we're judgmental with ourselves for being judgmental. Or there are feelings coming up in the body we can't make room for." Rather than insisting on a "rosy view of reality, where we just 'buck up' and have an optimistic view," he suggests instead that this is about "realism" and "really training awareness to look at All of Life—everything that's happening moment to moment."

Healing reflection: How well are you able to push back on thoughts and relate to them only as thoughts, rather than automatically as reality or your identity? And have you ever been able to relate to changing emotions inside like weather patterns overhead?

Antidepressant lifestyle challenge: Learn to push back on thoughts and emotions enough to observe them without interference—even if it takes practice! Look up Jon Kabat-Zinn's body-scan for depression recovery and give it a try before bed one evening.

7. Nurturing connections: Building deeper relationships and strengthening emotional support networks.

On their own, most people don't seem to be able to find what they need to heal. As Mendek said, "Using willpower alone, I was unable to change these patterns. Battling my thoughts made me their prisoner, and resisting my emotions energized them."

The support of others made a significant difference in many stories—with the healing power of authentic human connection showing up often in recovery narratives. This aligns with research showing that social isolation is harmful, while meaningful relationships buffer against stress and bolster resilience. What's striking is that for many, the quality of connections mattered more than quantity—even one person who truly "saw" them made a profound difference.

Opening up to receive others' support.

Crystal was in a bad enough place that she decided she couldn't leave her church meeting "without someone knowing what was going on." After opening up, she was included regularly by those concerned for her: "These people didn't just put on events as some church gimmick—they actually cared about one another."

Jennifer notes, "It takes incredible courage to reach out for help when the tools you have are no longer working."

Nicole describes her community's support as well: "I felt loved—it was a place of belonging. I found an open, friendly, shoulder to cry on to talk with people about my desperate feelings."

Jane attended an Emotions Anonymous (EA) meeting as a "last ditch effort to find some measure of relief," saying, "For the first time in my life, I felt real hope. I was not alone! They care for me in times of illness. They lend me their strength when I don't have enough of my own."

Not as easy as it looks.

Opening up, however, doesn't guarantee a positive result. When Julie was at her "wits end" with depression, she recalls her friends being "incredibly supportive" when she opened up about not knowing "what to do." This left her family as well "in a state of complete fear"—"afraid that I may try and hurt myself."

Though active support is valuable, Thomas speaks of the importance of letting relationships breathe: "There is a real power in reserving some time, day by day, for not doing anything . . . Not fixating on these problems coming up. We fall into these ruts so quickly, where 'this person is depressed, we need to make them not depressed.'"

Providing this kind of relationship space is different from unhealthy isolation, where "disconnection spirals into more disconnection." Johann came to believe that depression is "itself a form of grief—for all the connections we need, but don't have." To counter this trend in his own life, he describes proactively "spend[ing] much more time face-to-face" with those he loved, reporting being "more deeply connected" now than he "ever [has] been before."

Receiving love.

Johann says, "You're not going to be able to deal with this problem alone."

Marsha describes a friend who was "always there for [her], always ready to listen, again and again and again, always giving comfort," emphasizing how this "kept [her] alive."

The impact of such loving support is especially apparent in times when someone is desperate.

In one dire moment, Ben describes standing on a bridge ready to take his life, but recalls how a stranger in a light-brown jacket stayed close. "He wasn't particularly comforting, or deep, or intentional. He was just there. He didn't try to tell me that everything would be okay. He didn't give me any of the empty

> motivational platitudes." Instead, the man "asked [Ben] about [his] life." Ben continues, "It was comforting to have someone stand with me. The little I said, he heard. He saw me. He didn't leave. Maybe it's because he stayed—I did too."

Yet, like everything described here, connection isn't a panacea.

> "Even with new friends and church activities," Crystal notes, "the darkness was still trying to lure me back into the deafening silence of isolation."

Creative ways to connect.

What about those who struggle to find someone?

> Grant, immersing himself in the history of his family, gradually noticed that he began to feel "lighter"—to the point that he "didn't even notice the depression at all."
>
> Nothing reached Julie until she adopted a golden retriever puppy, who became a healing place "without ridicule, doubt, sorrow, or anger."
>
> Another person describes a pet's love as uniquely involving "no judgment or criticism, just unconditional love on a continuous level."

Healing reflection: How connected do you feel to people you trust to be supportive, understanding, and kind? Are there people from your past that you could reach out to in order to expand your circle and network of friends right now?

Antidepressant lifestyle challenge: Reach out regularly to people you love and trust—asking about their lives and letting them know about your own. Pick one person you haven't spoken with in a while who's been this kind of support in the past and send them a note or call them.

8. Healing past wounds: Embracing forgiveness and working through traumatic experiences.

What we've been through in the past most definitely impacts our present, even when we're not ready to see that.

> "I didn't talk at all about the violence and abuse I survived as a child until I was in my mid-twenties," Johann says.
>
> Sarah admits that when she eventually "felt able to share with others the details of her father's abuse, I was close to a panic attack. It surprised me how hard it was to talk about my experiences, even though [others] had told me about their own abuses."

Even when able to verbalize them, memories can still be fuzzy.

> "As a child, teenager, and adult, the first ten years of my life had been mostly erased. There were no memories of sexual abuse, but my body never forgot and replayed the disgusting events every night in the form of nightmares and night terrors."

Trauma leaves lasting imprints in our bodies and minds. Research on adverse childhood experiences (ACEs) shows that early trauma significantly increases the risk of mental and physical health problems throughout life. Yet, while the past cannot be changed, our relationship to it can transform dramatically. This work isn't quick or easy, as reflected in these stories, but for many it was an essential part of lasting recovery.

Emotional freedom from the effects of abuse.

> Sarah describes eventually learning to stand back from her life and see how she could "extricate" herself from the "wreckage" of her past—allowing her to "stand beside it" so she "could view it more objectively."
>
> "I hadn't made my father do anything. He was the abuser; I was the child," she says. "The abuse no longer controlled me as much. I learned to respond more and react less."
>
> Moni describes becoming able to forgive her abusive father, who had died nineteen years earlier, "for all the pain he had caused

[her] as a child." As a result, she says, "it was as if a heavy curtain was drawn back from the window of my soul."

When "forgiveness" is not enough.

"Because I'd wanted to be a good Christian, I had 'forgiven' my father," Sarah recalls from her childhood, "when he asked for forgiveness for having been 'a little fresh.'" Later in her healing process, she learned that forgiveness "has to be accompanied by an appreciation and understanding of what has happened and the impact of it on your life."

"I forgave my parents because hating them was hurting me," another individual says. "I am slowly building a relationship with my father based on mutual honesty and respect."

While reconciliation can help, sometimes separation is needed for healing.

After years of "living in an abusive marriage filled with sorrow and pain," Helen describes divorce from her abusive husband as crucial to healing.

Another woman who had been "horribly abused" describes how some of "these deep hurts can take years, decades, to work through." She adds her belief that "some wounds will never completely go away in this life." Instead, she suggests we "can learn to embrace them in forgiveness."

Removing the burden of toxic anger.

"One day I will die," Mendek writes. "[And] before my last breath leaves my body, I don't want to carry my bitterness and venom to the grave."

Marianne Williamson once said, "Unforgiveness is like drinking poison and waiting for the other person to die." But knowing how to release those toxic emotions isn't always so easy:

Even while seeing the clear impact of her parents' actions on her life, Sarah describes a profound moment where she was able to say, "Forgive them, Father; they did not know what they were doing." She reflects, "The person who wounded you is not hurt by your unforgiveness, but you are. I had to learn how to let go of all the hurt and unforgiveness. Nothing that hindered my healing process could remain."

A woman realized how she had over-blamed her mother and father, saying, "In all honesty, my parents only did what they knew how to do, and I totally get it, because that's what I'm doing now as a parent. We work with the tools we have."

Another person reflects, "I was finally able to see my father in his true light, and feelings of compassion and understanding flowed out of me toward him."

"I was tired of hating the world," Melissa says. "I was tired of seeing it in fogged lenses that only magnified the world's bleakness and darkness." She concludes, "The world was full of beautiful people," including so many who had "endured their own version of suffering."

Reseeing the pain.

Pain is one thing. Our explanation and interpretation for it is another:

"The story we tell ourselves about our past experiences dictates how we feel about them," Alexi Pappas says.

"It's not the things we remember that define us," Mark says, "but the stories we tell ourselves about the things we think we remember."

"We experience pain when we encounter trauma, hurt, or loss," Brooke explains, "but we perpetuate suffering by what we tell ourselves about what happened." Brooke then describes how painful events can "become integrated into our greater life narrative" bringing freedom and "cleansing."

Healing reflection: Is there anything from your past that weighs on you, draining you of sweetness and preventing you from feeling the love, peace, and joy you want to feel? If so, what steps have you taken to heal in the past that have been helpful—and what more can you do in the future?

Antidepressant lifestyle challenge: Take some time to write a list of things that are weighing you down onto a piece of paper. Consider sharing something on the list with someone you trust—exploring ways to keep it in the past for good. Even if it feels scary, take a deep breath and send a message to this person to get started.

9. Discovering purpose: Expanding your sense of meaning, identity, and connection to others.

We've found in our statistical analyses that one of the strongest predictors of depression is how much meaning and purpose people feel (or don't feel) in their lives. In addition to receiving love, people who had found deeper emotional healing also spoke repeatedly about rediscovering the joy of giving and sharing love. This included tangible relationships in their own communities, along with spiritual experiences.

The search for meaning and purpose isn't a luxury—it's a fundamental human need. Psychiatrist Viktor Frankl observed in Nazi concentration camps that those who maintained a sense of purpose were more likely to survive.[7] Modern research confirms this: a strong sense of purpose correlates with reduced depression risk, better physical health outcomes, and even longer lifespan. For many in our study, finding purpose involved self-transcendence and connection to something larger than themselves.

Getting outside of your head.

One individual says, "In my isolation, I was stuck inside of my head, focusing on myself most of the time."

Johann likewise acknowledges the self-absorption often common with depression: "You become trapped in your own story and your own thoughts, and they rattle around in your head with a dull, bitter insistence."

He continues, "If you want to stop being depressed, don't fixate on how you're worth it. It's thinking about you, you, you that's helped to make you feel so lousy. The real path to happiness comes from letting yourself flow into other people's stories and letting their stories flow into yours."

Other experiences show a similar pattern:

Crystal says, "Volunteering was pivotal in learning how to get my eyes off of myself and start considering others."

Linda reflects, "My healing came through connection, it came through motivating and encouraging others and it came through making an impact in people's lives."

The motivation of newfound purpose.

Johann emphasizes, "Everybody wants to feel useful, and have purpose. . . . [People] want to feel like they've had an impact on other humans—that they've improved the world."

The impact of making a difference kept showing up:

"Creating, giving, sharing, and connecting gave me reasons to get out of bed each morning," Melissa says, "and defined why I was here."

"Losing myself in love is my best self-care and healing prescription," another person says. "Pouring myself into others lifts my spirits, turns my mind and heart, and brings relief and sustaining packets of joy."

After finally becoming emotionally "unstuck," Ben felt like he was "making up for lost time" like Scrooge. Nothing excited him more than the possibility that he "might really be able to help people."

One woman describes the impact of "playing happily" with her two children, seeing "this peace and comfort and love in their life," and "how different" it was from her own.

Another woman speaks of what motivated her to keep going: "I was important to my daughter. I loved doing all of the things with her that my mother had never done with me. We read together, which became a part of her nighttime ritual. We said prayers before bed and then I would kiss her goodnight. I always tried to listen [as she told] me about her day. All of this was immensely healing. Knowing I was important to [my daughter] gave me strength."

Johann also suggests that "happiness is really feeling like you've impacted another human positively. . . . If you can be happy for others . . . vicarious joy is going to be available millions of ways every single day."

Discovering a new source of confidence, comfort, and connection.

Spirituality helped many in this healing process.

"The dark night of the soul is the place where one is invited into a deeper, more transformative relationship with the divine," one individual says.

After feeling "parched by life, sucked dry," Juanita describes being humbled and grateful to feel herself "in the presence of God who was quenching in me a thirst that only God could satisfy"—helping her to once again "know what it meant to be fully alive."

People have very different experiences of spirituality, with some feeling challenged by faith. Many people seek deeper healing outside of any faith tradition. In most healing stories we reviewed, however, people reported being helped by engaging on a deeper level with spiritually transcendent practices, especially when they felt stuck:

"I acknowledge I don't have the strength," Aaron recalls—describing a moment when his emotional burdens were so "heavy" they were "crushing" him.

Juanita also admits, "My life was taken down to the bones . . . I had come to the end of myself. It all crumbled."

Nicole ultimately began to "cry out to God" to save her from the pain "because I didn't know what else to do."

This is when many described the impact of a deepened spiritual connection:

"My roommate and I read the Bible cover to cover for the first time," Crystal says. "This was the most transforming year of my life, and the healing was so drastic that I consider it an emotional death to life miracle."

Juanita describes coming to a "deep, loving union with God" involving "the kind of peace spoken of by those who have experienced a near-death episode." He continues, "I was surrounded by love I had never experienced, love that was dense and filled the space all around me, that fed the deepest part of my starved soul."

"My eyes were opened to creation itself—"rocks, clouds" another person says. "God . . . engaged in my heart. . . . A euphoric joy came upon me."

In her story of seeking healing from depression, one Muslim woman described Allah as "the One who sends the relief. No matter how bad it gets, He will always be there to catch us and offer us solace." Her experience has taught her that "everything else falls into place" when she turns her heart towards God, quoting the Quran as stating "it is in the remembrance of Allah that the hearts find peace"—along with another author describing Allah as "the only One who can release us and make us whole again."[8]

Knowing you're not alone.

Lucie, in a moment of desperate pain, asked her brother to pray for her. "I don't remember what he said, but I remember feeling this warmth on my physical body as if someone was wrapping me in love—as if I was being hugged. That's the Lord's way of telling me that He was still there for me, and He loved me."

She continues, "After two and a half years of turmoil, pain, of grief, of feeling lost, I awoke the next morning feeling the same love—the same unconditional love, safety, comfort, and direction."

"The thought of there being a God who was in control of everything was a comforting feeling for me," Nicole says. "I then didn't need to worry as much and do everything on my own."

After a sacred experience of pure love, Mendek says that "for the first time," he "believed that the world was a kind and magnificent place."

Aligning with something bigger than yourself.

Juanita feels grateful her mind and body "shut me down, stopped me dead in my tracks. I had to stop believing that I was strong enough to pull myself out" and "stop believing that my intellect would get me through this."

"Even the whole world—and everything in it—can't help me," Aaron recollects. Then looking upward, he says, "But you can," and refers to a scripture: "My grace is sufficient."

One Jewish woman described how her faith "took her out of her depression" as her religion taught her that "every person is, in fact, special" and "Everybody has a unique mission."[9]

Several people spoke of the impact of making changes and repenting.

One man emphasized the importance of "congruence," or "living in harmony with core life values and aspirations," which helped to bring again "peace, joy, and love" in his life.

After getting baptized in a Christian church, one woman experienced "a real inner peace and strength." Immediately out of the water, she says, "I began to smile. My smile began within me and didn't stop at my face."

Seeking, even when you're not feeling it.

This spiritual growth is not simply a one-time occasion, with people describing the value of "spiritual practice" and "spiritual nourishment."

Nicole notes having "ongoing heavenly encounters on a regular basis" through scripture and prayer. "Doing this on a daily basis, I started receiving peace."

One Muslim woman shared gratitude for the "many chances throughout the day to come close to Allah"—describing how she even started waking up earlier "to get the blessings of praying while everyone else sleeps." As she "reestablished" habits connecting her with God, she writes: "slowly, slowly, I started feeling more like myself again."[10]

"I had to accept sometimes feeling disconnected, without supposing it must mean something was wrong in my life," Mark said about his "spiritual dailies." That meant continuing to seek and practice "even if [you] can't always feel" the benefits.

Healing reflection: How much of a connection do you feel in your life to a purpose, passion, or person bigger than yourself? When in the past have you felt this kind of connection—and what would you be open to trying to feel more of that spiritual foundation for your emotional healing?

Antidepressant lifestyle challenge: Experiment with different ways to center your life on something or someone greater than yourself, including people, purposes, and passions you care about. Consider a spiritual practice others have found helpful in deepening their own sense of meaning, purpose, and identity. If you can't think of anything, start praying each night or morning—sharing openly what's on your heart with as much faith as you can muster.

10. Expanding emotional autonomy: Increasing personal freedom and reducing long-term dependencies.

Looking more long-term, the stories of lasting healing we've gathered often describe reduced dependence on external substances or interventions as making a difference for their emotional healing.

This journey toward autonomy—the ability to regulate and care for oneself without excessive and unhealthy dependence on external substances or interventions—emerged as a final important theme in recovery stories. While various substances, drugs, and medications can provide genuine benefits for emotional challenges, particularly in the short-term, the development of more emotional self-reliance seems to ultimately support more sustainable healing and independence.

Reducing long-term reliance on alcohol and illegal drugs.

Repeatedly, people spoke of reducing or eliminating alcohol as part of their healing.

> "I realized the drinking was a slow suicide," says one person. "I had really become very reliant on it. So, when I put the drink down, I was faced with the reality of my life. However, in a matter of weeks, my life just started to clear up a little bit. I no longer felt totally controlled by my emotions. All of a sudden, I felt this sense of hope."

Other rippling effects.

> "I immediately noticed that I can't tolerate dating the men in my life without drinking," Brooke says. Previously, she describes "getting drunk, sleeping with men who desire me, but do not have the capacity to love me, and in the morning waking up and dragging myself to class." At first, it felt "liberating to rebel against [her] religious past." But noticing how much alcohol and casual sex altered her mood," Brooke cries, "This is not the freedom I crave."
>
> After many years of drinking and medicating, Angel relates what happened as she began to taper: "I had been hopeless for so many years. My world had become so small that I didn't see any light at the end of the tunnel—and all of a sudden, as I started getting sober from alcohol and getting off these medications, I just started to feel a little bit of emotional energy—and hope."

Reducing long-term reliance on prescription medications.

While alcohol and illegal drugs are clearly different from substances legally prescribed, some common themes of emotional dependence upon a prescribed substance do exist.

> After describing all the medications he was taking, one man admits, "I felt crappy all the time. I couldn't sleep well at night. I felt suspicious of people, nervous, hopeless, and tired."
>
> One woman started taking antidepressants after developing postpartum depression, "which began a 14-year-long saga of medication usage and adjustment."
>
> Another woman tried "talk therapy and almost every mood stabilizer and antidepressant on the market." She says, "they worked for a while, but the symptoms always came back and increased."

To be clear, others were grateful for the past impact of medical treatment, even if they eventually tapered off medication.

> Stephanie says, "They brought me back into enough of a state of equilibrium that my soul could commence healing."

> Charlotte relates, “It does not take away the despair, but it takes the edge off. I intuitively understand it is a temporary fix.”
>
> Another woman says, “The medication I was prescribed was absolutely necessary and saved my life. It brought me through the darkest part of my journey. It was a necessary stepping-stone and now I have stepped off.”

For some, the initial boost from the medication was so significant that they don’t feel right about ever tapering off.

> For example, one woman says, “After it kicked in [and] actually started working, and I feel normal again. And I’ve had no recurrence of symptoms for two years. And I plan to keep it that way. And, I have no plans to get off the medication any time soon. It’s working for me, and I don’t want to mess with what’s working.”

New realizations.

> After mentioning how medications helped initially, one man says, “I realized I didn’t care whether I was alive, or about my girlfriend or my faith.”
>
> Another recalls, “Most of the medication either caused severe side effects or they made me feel dull, which I could not accept because I enjoy being an active person. I had always been extremely conscientious about taking my medication. For a long time, I believed that the meds would help me get better if only I could find the right one. Finally, I realized that, despite the medications, I was getting sicker, had less energy and more anxiety every year. The medications were only helping a few symptoms but weren’t solving the problem.”
>
> After describing how “a doctor tried to put [her] on antidepressants,” Gwen remembers thinking, “If I need them, then yes, I’ll come back to it, but I wanna first try [other options].”

A decision that can feel scary.

Part of the fear of tapering is tied to a social stigma of not taking medication.

Influenced by what they called "a changed belief about myself and what I began to entertain as possible for me," one person starts to take gradual steps to get off meds they had been taking for years.

One woman relates, "I was afraid to drop the meds, I was literally told in the beginning that I would probably be on medication for the rest of my life. Even though I knew my brain was healing, what if I was wrong about it?" She continues, "It was so scary for me. I never want to feel that darkness and pain again." After praying and counseling with her husband, she described feeling peace about tapering very gradually, while watching together carefully for any signs of trouble.

Slow and steady wins the race.

In most cases, going off medication too quickly can make withdrawal effects worse.

Michael says, "I definitely do not recommend stopping a medication without talking to a doctor first."

Another person suggests, "It is a mistake to try to go off of medications by yourself, especially if you have been on them for as long as I had!"

One individual, who felt his body had become "desensitized" to the psychiatric medications he was taking, decided they "really weren't working anymore." His doctor "stated that [he] still needed to come off the medications slowly because [his] body needed to detox from them and coming off of powerful medications too quickly could be dangerous."

With professional support, another person says, "I was able to wean off all my medications within four months."

Another person admits, "Since the psychiatrist 'wouldn't have approved' of even [my] gentle and gradual tapering plan, I did it all without [her]. She told me I needed to be on medications for the rest of my life. She was wrong. . . . My former psychiatrist would be astonished to see how happy and healthy I am today."

A good professional may still express concerns, while affirming the individual's right to decide for themselves.

> "When I told both my therapist and psychiatrist of my choice, they were concerned to say the least, but absolutely supportive."
>
> Another says, "I remember my psychiatrist saying, 'If you're going to do this, you will need two things: exercise and laughter.'"

Navigating some turbulence.

After a transformative period of learning, Moni admits, "I felt that the medication was not needed anymore. For the first time in my life, I felt settled, calm, and peaceful."

David describes life changes leading him to a place of readiness: "My energy levels increased amazingly as I continued with my new diet and exercise regime, and I continued to meditate and work at finding peace with my situation. Within two short months, I found myself staring at the box of Prozac as I had a little 'farewell' conversation with it."

This kind of mindful taper involves ongoing watchfulness in how the body and mind is responding, which can lead to adjustments in the tapering approach.

> As one woman recalls, "In the past, when I would taper my antidepressant medication, I experienced unpleasant symptoms, during the withdrawal process, such as mood swings, suicidal thoughts, severe PMS, difficulty making decisions, and lack of confidence in myself." However, this time when she tapered, "using an integrated approach of diet, nutritional supplements, and meditation," she reports that over a gradual reduction over five months, "[she] did not experience any withdrawal symptoms, and [she] was able to continue to work full time."

It's important to note that similar reductions in dependency sometimes happen with alternative interventions as well.

> One person recounts, "I have gradually been able to decrease the amount of nutritional supplements necessary for maintaining my health."

Feeling myself again.

Challenges naturally continue for many people.

> "With my doctor's help I have now been off of the depression meds for almost 3 months," Stephanie says. "And I feel like I think we are supposed to feel as people!" This didn't mean things were "blissful" she admits, but she has learned to experience some emotional "turbulence" while knowing how to "navigate [her] way around it and sometimes through it."
>
> Having been medication-free for almost two years, one person says, "Is it easy? No. It is a challenge every day. But I choose this challenge."

Different people have different experiences. Others have found positive places staying on their medications.

> David, after tapering off the antidepressants he had been on for fourteen years, describes feeling "intellectually at [his] best."
>
> In describing their family's positive experience tapering, Carrie says, "[For] anyone who has that still, small, but persistent voice in their heads telling them there has to be a better way, there is. We are living it, amazed at the difference in our family."

Healing reflection: Are you currently feeling dependent on any kind of substance for your day-to-day emotional well-being? If that's what you need right now, you'll feel that. And if you need to make an adjustment, you'll feel that too. Do you trust your intuition to guide you to what is right for you?

Antidepressant lifestyle challenge: If your well-being depends long-term on a substance of any kind, think seriously on what it would look like to taper off mindfully and safely over time. Think about who can be part of your support team in this process.

Conclusion: The Journey Continues

While we've examined these ten themes individually, in real life they form an interconnected web of healing practices. Progress in one area naturally supports growth in others. For example, better sleep (nourishing the body) improves your ability to regulate emotions (mindful awareness), which enhances your connections with others (nurturing relationships).

What's particularly encouraging about these patterns is their accessibility. Unlike treatments requiring special credentials or expensive resources, many of these healing practices are available to anyone willing to take small, consistent steps. This democratization of mental health recovery offers additional hope to those who may have felt that healing was beyond their reach.

The stories we've collected also reveal that healing isn't about achieving perfection or completely eliminating life's challenges. One woman admits that emotional turbulence "sometimes still hits." Michael says, "Of course, I still have moods, but they are normal moods, not the wild swings as before."

"My wife and I still know that my Eeyore self is there, but we try to keep [him] at a 'lovable and livable' level," Mark reflects—describing how he uses six key lifestyle steps taped inside his kitchen cupboard and if feeling "a little off" he can check the list and say, "Ah, I'm not sleeping well. Time to soak in some sunlight to set my body clock."

True healing involves developing a new relationship with our challenges—one characterized by resilience, wisdom, and the knowledge that we have tools to navigate whatever arises. Each of these ten themes represents not just a step toward recovery but a lifelong practice that continues to deepen over time.

The path to lasting mental health may not be quick or linear, but these stories demonstrate that with persistence, patience, and creativity, profound transformation is possible.

Chapter 6

Patterns in Lasting Freedom from Addiction

In this chapter, we'll focus on the experience of those who have found (at long last) enduring freedom from sexual compulsivity and pornography use. Many of the individuals whose experiences we share below reference their religious or moral convictions during their stories of recovery.

Religious tradition can shape how people feel about pornography, and the reasons they believe it's a problem in the first place. Still, there are many people who don't believe pornography is morally wrong or contrary to divine law, but they feel a similar desire to quit or reduce porn usage after seeing the negative impact of porn in their lives and relationships. These stories of recovery can apply to people of diverse religious (or non-religious) backgrounds, as well as to those struggling with other compulsive behavior (such as drug and alcohol usage, or even shopping or gaming).

What better place to look for clarity about lasting healing than from the experiences of people who have actually found it?

We wanted to know what went into this healing. Through

published memoirs, online YouTube accounts, and other public writing, as well our own interviews, we gathered addiction recovery stories that showed clear evidence of lasting freedom—after a period of compulsive struggle.

Although they still had challenging days, each person whose story we used in this analysis was clearly in a different place than before. "I'm not foolish enough to think I'm ever completely safe," Tony says, "yet I finally have hope that I can stay out of the mire in which I previously stayed."

Before diving into individual recovery elements, consider what differentiates addiction from other mental health challenges: its distinctive cycle of tolerance, withdrawal, preoccupation, and loss of behavioral control. Recovery must address each component of this cycle, which is why comprehensive approaches show consistently better outcomes than single-focus interventions.

Here are the ten key themes that stood out from those who have found more sustainable healing and freedom from pornography addiction:

1. **Owning your recovery:** Acknowledging struggles honestly and taking responsibility for your healing path forward.
2. **Renewing hope:** Believing in the possibility of lasting freedom and letting this hope fuel your recovery journey.
3. **Seeking new knowledge:** Embracing learning as a tool for growth and healing by exploring fresh perspectives.
4. **Embracing openness:** Cultivating honesty and vulnerability in relationships in order to build more trust and accountability.
5. **Healing lingering wounds:** Working through deeper pain from the past that can drive relief seeking in the present.
6. **Practicing mindfulness:** Observing thoughts and urges like weather patterns overhead—calm and without judgment.
7. **Creating structure:** Designing daily routines and establishing healthy boundaries that support sobriety.
8. **Learning to be consistent:** Investing patiently in steady, daily efforts—rather than quick fixes—for lasting recovery.

9. **Serving others:** Turning attention outward by helping those in need and finding purpose beyond oneself.
10. **Exploring spirituality:** Tapping into faith practices that provide comfort, strength, and a sense of identity.

Many of these same themes show up prominently in the broader research literature touched on in chapter 3, as well as our own quantitative reviews in chapter 5. While our focus is primarily on pornography and sexual compulsivity, these patterns have shown remarkable consistency across different types of addictions. For instance, these same themes appear consistently across recovery from alcohol, drug, gambling, and food addictions—demonstrating that lasting healing arises not through willpower and controlling problematic behaviors alone, but through the larger practices and patterns of one's life, heart, and mind.

From our study of other forms of addiction, it's clear these patterns have relevance and applicability to other compulsive habits too, including chemical dependency. It appears as if underlying principles of recovery transcend any specific substance or behavior, revealing universal truths about human healing and transformation.

1. Owning your recovery: Acknowledging struggles honestly and taking responsibility for your healing path forward.

It's very common for people to deny the full reality of what they're facing and resist taking full responsibility for it too. Those who find lasting freedom are eventually willing to do both. "To me, I just thought it was a bad habit. I never thought of it as an addiction," admits Stephen, until arriving at a new awareness of just how "out of control" it was.

This transition from minimization to honest recognition typically reflects a growing awareness of how serious the problem really is.

- "I told myself it was just a harmless habit, that I could end it if I wanted or needed to end it, but I was deceiving myself," says Neal.
- "I didn't think it was wrong," Chantel admits, with Matt adding, "I justified in my mind that it wasn't cheating," before something "opened my eyes to the destruction in my life."
- This awareness can happen privately through difficult moments, like Neal reports: "Eventually, my wife walked in on me. My self-deception ended and I admitted that I really had a problem."

This pivotal shift from denial to ownership represents the true beginning of recovery for many. More than simply an acknowledgement that the problem exists, this is about accepting personal agency in both the problem and its solution. All this contrasts sharply with the passive victimhood often characterizing active addiction—the sense of being entirely powerless, and inescapably controlled by forces beyond one's influence.

Owning the healing process.

- Stephen describes letting his wife shoulder the burden of his recovery, with her willingness to say, "I have got to help my husband deal with this problem." He later took his own responsibility saying, "Never give the impression [to a partner] that their behavior or their body shape or their sexuality in the bedroom is responsible for a man betraying the relationship."

> **Recovery Temperature Check:** On a scale of 1-10, how honestly have you faced the full reality of your struggle? What would it take to move that number up by one point?

Anti-addiction lifestyle challenge: Write a letter to yourself detailing the specific ways your addiction has impacted your life and relationships. Be honest and compassionate. Then, list three concrete steps you can take this week to begin addressing these issues—including potentially speaking with someone you trust about what you're facing.

2. Renewing hope: Believing in the possibility of lasting freedom and letting this hope fuel your recovery journey.

It's easy for those feeling stuck to give up hope.

> "After 50+ years, I didn't think anything would work, I was too far gone," Larry says. After being introduced to the 12-steps, he recalls, "For the first time in a long time, I had this thing called hope."

Hope in addiction recovery often functions differently than in other contexts. It must be both aspirational enough to motivate change yet pragmatic enough to withstand disappointment. Recovery stories reveal a distinctive form of "clear-eyed hope" that acknowledges difficulty while maintaining faith in the possibility of transformation.

> Dave describes becoming convinced that he was "stuck" in the problem and "could not overcome it."
>
> When he sought spiritual help "to lead [him] and heal me," Matt spoke of feeling "lighter . . . there was a weight lifted off my shoulders. Like there was hope."

This hope can grow more after signs of real improvement.

> After finally facing urges and triggers "without giving in,"

- Vinny says, "With each little success, my hope and confidence increased."
- Jessica describes the "joy that came" after experiencing her first "porn-free break"—feeling like, "I can do it!"
- "Wow, I don't have these urges anymore," another remembers realizing. "It felt so good.'"

Throughout people's stories, they turn to offer encouragement to others.

- One man who had been walking in freedom for three and half years, shares, "My marriage . . . has never been better. . . . If you are currently struggling in this area, *this can be your story.*"
- "I know that this journey towards freedom isn't easy," Taylor shares about her own journey sparked by spiritual encouragement, "but I truly believe that freedom is possible for every single one of [us]! Don't give up on yourself, keep fighting."

Recovery Temperature Check: What's one specific evidence of progress, however small, that you can identify in your recovery journey? How might focusing on this evidence strengthen your hope?

Anti-addiction lifestyle challenge: Expand your hope by researching and reaching out to a local recovery support group or online community. Attend a meeting to hear stories of successful recovery. Write down three inspiring takeaways from what you learn.

3. Seeking new knowledge: Embracing learning as a tool for growth and healing by exploring fresh perspectives.

Learning appears to be a near universal part of people's healing and recovery journeys.

Roger speaks of making "a bunch of self-discoveries" during his recovery process, thanks to support organizations, online lectures, and spiritual readings.

Jorge describes the discovery of the Fortify app as "the start of my real recovery"—saying, "I learned so much from the training and was encouraged by the forums that I wasn't alone! I went on a 7-month streak."

Effective recovery learning follows the "know-feel-do" progression: Intellectual understanding leads to emotional recognition, which enables behavioral change. Those achieving lasting freedom describe this integration of knowledge across all three domains, rather than compartmentalizing what they learned.

One man describes a "steep and rapid growth curve" in his recovery journey, with every week bringing some kind of "revelation about myself, about my past patterns, and about what needed to change in my heart."

Renewing and rewiring thought.

"Belief in God alone cannot immediately reverse an addiction," Nick says, even as a man of faith. "We have to rewire our thinking."

After being stuck in what he called a "death grip" for fifteen years, Eric experienced a "transformation" as he changed the way he thought.

Roger describes jettisoning "some of the faulty core beliefs" he had.

And Timothy describes working "so that I do not even think pornographically."

Understanding biological forces.

Brett says, "Sexual addiction is not just a moral problem; it is also a brain problem. . . . A powerful chemical neurotransmitter called dopamine, or the 'gotta have it' molecule, is released in our brains."

Recognizing deeper patterns.

"There are roots for everything we do," Taylor says.

"If a tree represented our life [and] someone were to cut our trunk and look at the roots underneath . . . what would they find?" asks Vinny B.—who describes "working more on preventing my unwanted behaviors by dealing with the underlying issues instead of waiting until I was in a crisis and then trying to resist acting out."

Education is not enough.

Matt warns those who "want to think ourselves into the right action," cautioning that "our relationship with porn has been honed over years of repeated involvement. We have conditioned ourselves by returning to it, over and over."

For that reason, he says, "any useful knowledge we acquire is quickly overridden by our own desire and cravings," with a "big difference between being aware of a problem and deciding to change."

That's why the AA Big Book famously says, "self-knowledge availed us nothing."

As Matt puts it, "our knowledge alone cannot change us," and "we won't be able to think our way out of this." To those presuming that if they "find the right article or idea," they'll "do the right thing," he gently suggests that they may be trying to find "a less painful way to quit" with this mindset, namely, "one that doesn't involve giving up things we like, looking bad, or asking for help."

Seeing people, not objects.

Tony describes a moment when he "saw through the façade [and] illusion" in a video he was watching. "It was only a second, a glimpse." But it was enough to realize that "porn is an act—a lie."

John likewise describes the impact of realizing that the woman he "used to look at is made in the image and likeness of God—she's some daddy's little girl, she's precious to God." He admits, "When that revelation hit my heart, I could no longer look at a girl as a piece of meat, or as something for pleasure for me."

"Think for a moment about the reality that these are real people, many with tormented pasts and very painful childhoods, who have had that pain exploited," Joshua says, underscoring "how the porn industry many times takes people who are vulnerable (abused), and sometimes even homeless or runaways, and exploits them," with additional pain "once they are inside the industry."

When he realized these women were "hurting, desperate, in need of help and protection," that insight "startled" him. He says, "The mask fell off. The women were no longer objects. They were real women with sometimes torturous pasts and vulnerable pain."

"That knowledge changed me," Joshua continues. "From that moment forward, my addiction was only a few months away from being completely washed away."

Understanding love versus exploitation.

Dave recollects coming to see more clearly "the false concept of love" that essentially defined "love as what porn is," and it keeps hinting that "everyone is having sex with everyone else." Since even the women being mistreated "looked happy."

Jessica recalls how she used to believe that "true happiness was found in sex."

"That's not real love," another came to learn.

Vinny describes the power of coming to see and appreciate a "whole person as opposed to narrowly focusing on body parts," emphasizing the value of seeing "sexual thoughts and urges" as a "normal, healthy part of life and how harnessing and directing those urges is the key."

Transforming beyond intellectual knowledge.

"It's not truth that will keep us from deception," John points out, "It's the love of truth. When you want that in the innermost parts of your heart more than you want anything else."

"The word of God needs to go from our minds to our hearts," he summarizes. "I used to have a desire for pornography—I could be enticed," he says. But "once the word gets into your heart, the deep places of our heart, everything changes."

"When I see that now, I'm repulsed by that." Compared to a time when that "used to be like a magnet that would draw [him] in," John now says, "I don't have any desire for it."

Recovery Temperature Check: What's one insight about addiction that has significantly changed how you approach recovery?

Anti-addiction lifestyle challenge: Choose a reputable addiction recovery podcast or audiobook. Listen to it during your daily commute or while doing chores for one week. Then write down three new insights you've gained and how you plan to apply them.

4. Embrace openness: Cultivating honesty and vulnerability in relationships to build trust and accountability.

Many find power in sharing more openly with trusted people, with some saying, "I could not defeat this completely on my own," and "Becoming accountable to other trustworthy men was key for me."

> Jack speaks of "finding someone you trust who's not going to judge you but will help you make a change and ask you the difficult questions."
>
> "Were they taken aback?" Jackson remarks about people he shared details with. "Yes. Did they reject me? Not even for a moment. The people who love you will stand by you and help you get free."

Productive disclosure often follows a distinct pattern: initial sharing with a trusted individual, expanding to a small supportive group, and finally developing an ongoing life accountability practice.

Breaking free from secrecy.

> "I avoided telling people about my problem. I hid it from my wife. I tried to figure it out in secret," Matt says, admitting that he had "tried everything" except showing people what was actually happening.
>
> "I desperately did not want to come forward and get honest about it. I just wanted to stop," Stephen agrees.
>
> "Intimacy in a relationship can't exist with secrets," Vinny says.
>
> Neal adds, "Secrecy seems to be not only part of my sense of embarrassment," but also, "fuels the excitement."
>
> Jessica shares, "for me it was worth far more to keep face and keep the acceptance than it was to risk" others responses. Yet when one of her youth leaders admitted that she too "had been living a lie," Jessica was sure the leader would be condemned and

judged—but was, instead, dumbfounded when she witnessed her being "met with overwhelming joy and acceptance." She recalled being "completely stunned."

Before learning to share more fully what he was experiencing, Jason describes a time he only shared generically—just "enough"—resisting sharing fully what he was facing: "I thought that this thing was too dirty, too dark to share with anybody."

For Nick, confession to a trusted spiritual mentor became the beginning of his healing—something he sees as helping people "get real" about the places they've "worked so hard to hide" and "finally experience the kind of community that does transform us."

Mark adds: "When we open up our lives, we also give others permission to do the same."

Peer support makes a difference.

Joshua emphasizes how "important" it has been for him "to get involved with men or women who have overcome porn in the past."

Another says, "Just the act of being in a group and talking to guys who felt very similarly" was helpful.

About his group support, one man reflects, "It brought a lot of healing and hope—helped me feel it was possible."

Colby describes "building each other up with a sense of brotherhood" with other men "who knew everything about me" as central to successfully "walking in freedom for five years."

Phil says, "We know the good, the bad, and the ugly of each other. There are tears, there is tons of laughter, there is learning and growth."

Jorge found "live conversations with other guys in real time" and "being seen, and being there for others," as a "cornerstone" of his healing—"the regularity, the honesty and safety, the acceptance, and the acknowledgement that it is a journey." He adds, "It takes many repetitions of turning up defeated and feeling sure you're a failure and to be met with warmth, understanding, and encouragement to get back up, to start to unwork the old beliefs and lies that have long been held ("No one will love you if they know what you've done," etc.)."

"Having a couple of people who love and care for you even knowing about 'your junk' is so freeing!" Eric says, especially when they "ask you those tough questions" and aren't "afraid to step on our toes in a loving way."

Matt says accountability includes "making commitments in front of another human being." It means someone else knows what you are "actively committed to doing to stay porn free rather than just a passive commitment to not do a behavior."

Chantel advises, "Surround yourself with a community who understands that you want to quit—a community that wants to help you quit."

Finding the right support.

Many people describe various places of connection and accountability: regular group meetings, individual calls with others working recovery, teletherapy, spiritual mentors, and online accountability tools.

Recovery Temperature Check: What's one secret about your struggle that you've been hesitant to share? Who would be the safest person to begin this conversation with?

Anti-addiction lifestyle challenge: Identify a trusted person you can be open with. Set up a regular check-in where you can honestly discuss your progress, challenges, and goals.

5. Healing lingering wounds: Working through deeper pain from the past that can drive relief seeking in the present.

"We all have hurts in our lives," Eric says.

Colby says, "I didn't realize how intertwined life traumas and sexual actions were, and how they were connected."

Brett suggests asking yourself, "Where have I been wounded and how do those wounds affect me today? If we don't identify these wounds, we'll end up treating the symptoms rather than the root problems."

One man recalls sharing for the first time a secret he had held for fifteen years of being taken advantage of sexually as a teenager—describing revealing the truth as "a truly terrifying moment, but one that so needed to happen, to help bring freedom and healing to my very being."

Finding deeper healing.

This involves finding a deeper healing for those wounds than porn can ever provide:

"Most of the time there's a wounding in our heart," Eric notes, "and a lot of times we're medicating that wound in our heart with pornography."

Nick suggests that true freedom is the result of "learning to trust again" in your own relationships, rather than "simply convincing others to trust you." Adding that trust is rooted in a deeper confidence in a higher power, "the idea that no matter what happens we can depend on someone being there for us."

As a person of faith, Taylor describes allowing her higher power to "come into those dark, hidden, and hurting places," and learning to turn to spiritual sources of healing instead.

Understanding trauma's impact.

> "One of the largest reasons that a person becomes addicted to pornography," Nolan says, "is that they had a very damaging experience with intimacy and love sometime in either their distant or recent past."

Although it's important to not rush, healthy forgiveness clearly makes a tremendous difference for people—especially when considering the cost of holding onto major bitterness about the past.

> After even trained professionals failed to make a difference, Nolan admits, "because humans had hurt me my entire life, I couldn't trust humans." But "a simple cat who can at first seem aloof" made a huge difference, since that animal "didn't abandon me in the darkest moments of my soul when I really, really needed someone (or something) to love me despite all of the flaws."
>
> He reflects, "Once someone is able to truly feel real intimacy again, the urges to watch pornography start to disappear quite quickly, at least in my experience."

Recovery Temperature Check: Can you identify a specific emotional wound that your addictive behavior attempts to soothe or escape from? What healthier ways might address that same underlying need?

Anti-addiction lifestyle challenge: Start freewriting about anything painful in the past that still weighs on you emotionally. Consider sharing this with someone you trust—exploring additional ways to keep it in the past for good. Even if it feels scary, take a deep breath and take the next step.

6. Practicing mindfulness: Observing thoughts and urges like weather patterns overhead—calm and without judgment.

Learning a more gentle and creative way to approach thoughts and feelings was helpful in people's recoveries.

David says it made a "huge difference" in creating new, healthy patterns to grow in his "awareness of internal emotions and external triggers making [him] vulnerable" and "knowing how the body responds during addictive thinking."

Watching thoughts.

Dave describes thinking he was "helpless" anytime he got an alluring thought, which previously led him to believe, "I can't overcome it, so I might as well do it." Over time, he came to learn "that thought is not my thought," saying things like, "Nice try, devil. But you don't get me this time."

Seeing craving more clearly.

Rather than craving arising from "external sources like women and sexy TV shows," Matt describes craving as a "habit that came from within," starting with thoughts like "porn or a porn behavior would feel good right now."

"Sexual triggers start to have less power over you [when you] know what to do with them," Vinny says. "I remember during my heavy addiction years, whenever I would try to resist, [there was always a thought in the background], *You might as well give in to your urge because eventually you're going to do it anyway.*"

"Living as a free man, do the urges to view porn magically stop?" Dan asks, so you "never again feel the desire to watch porn?" Then he answers: "No." So if the urges don't completely stop, "What is freedom then? Freedom is knowing how to process those urges in a healthy, effective way. The difference is not whether you will have those urges. The difference is how you handle them. And the good news is, this is a skill that can be learned."

"I learned to successfully surf the urges," Roger says. "When the urges come, you're not concerned. You know exactly how to handle it. You've developed the skill to process the urge. You have a clear plan that works. And as time goes on, you get better and better at it. The more urges you process, the more you develop that skill (just like any skill!)."

Watching for triggers.

"I eliminated as many triggers as I could," Roger says. "I went through the materials I consumed [on] YouTube and I unfollowed the channels that were questionable to my value system. . . . I deleted [certain phone] numbers. . . . I purified the content in all of my social accounts."

"Think about when you're most triggered, whether it's a certain time of day, or after a certain situation," Taylor counsels.

Vinny suggests, "As we become aware of things that drive our setbacks, we *must* prepare a plan or strategy that reduces or eliminates that trigger." And you can "start to recognize when your sexual energy is heightened and you begin to refocus and redirect it to healthy outlets like physical exercise, improving relationships, being productive at work, pursuing interests and hobbies, and many more."

"What feelings or emotions most often trigger you? What are the most common thoughts or beliefs that go through your head that lead to craving?" one individual asks.

Recovery Temperature Check: When was the last time you experienced a strong urge but didn't act on it? What specific strategies helped you navigate that moment successfully?

Anti-addiction lifestyle challenge: Download the free Impact Suite app (or sign up online at ImpactSuite.com) and find the five-minute guided meditation focused on urge-surfing to practice several days. Use the Journaling feature to document how this practice affects your cravings and overall mood.

7. Creating structure: Designing daily routines and establishing healthy boundaries that support sobriety.

In addition to whatever internal changes of mind and heart are taking place, it's common to see people putting in place a system of discipline involving specific boundaries and behavioral patterns to guide wise choices. For many, a significant part of healing has been embracing or establishing some kind of "plan of action" or "gameplan."

It wasn't until Nick was introduced to a program of healing that helped him create a "plan of action," in collaboration with his wife, that freedom started to come.

Eric describes a "gameplan [he] could look at on paper" that he could "practically do to move towards freedom," which made him feel like he was "finally moving forward."

Finding structured support.

From personal plans, to online programs, to in-person faith ministries, to the 12-steps themselves, formalized programs were helpful guides for many to support recovery and nurture growth. Thoroughly structured plans and programs like Fortify and Freedom Fight that are well rounded and comprehensive and that look broadly across lifestyle were mentioned as especially helpful.

Creating a safe environment.

"When we're constantly living in an environment that's unsafe, it creates anxiety in us," Matt says, which itself can be an "emotional trigger." He then suggests, "Do everything you can to create safety in your home and in other areas you can control in your world"—trusting this safety will "lead to a calmer mind."

"What in your environment makes it easy to use porn?" one individual asks. "Whether it's our bedtime habits, our phones, our computers, our smart TVs, our streaming subscriptions, our social media—if porn is always a click away for us, it's hard to change our habits."

In his experience, Eliyahu says, "The desire to watch pornography will always win" since it is "such a powerful desire and feels so immediate." As a result, "each time the battle beg[an] tipping, even the slightest, in that direction," he would "always give in." He quotes the ancient Chinese war strategist Sun Tzu: "If your opponent is more powerful than you, avoid a confrontation." As reported in Ted Roberts' *Seven Pillars of Freedom* workbook, two MIT researchers concluded in a study that "Men's self-control when sexually aroused doesn't come from willpower but from avoiding situations in which one will become aroused and lose control."[1]

"Wherever the places are that you are most vulnerable," one man says, "make a plan to make it more difficult to watch porn in those places."

To illustrate, Nick says, "Putting off hard work became a means for porn to get in, so I have boundaries about how I work and study." Nick has also "chosen to limit [his] use of the internet, TV viewing, and cell phone use."

Mark got rid of R-rated and PG-13 movies and "certain magazines," while also keeping away from "television unless [he] was in the company of others.

Stephen similarly says, "I continuously take steps to separate myself from opportunities to make dumb choices."

Thomas admits that previously, "I didn't know what it meant to put boundaries and bottom lines in place and honestly abide by them."

Making positive commitments.

"To break a habit," says Craig Perra, creator of The Mindful Habit System for overcoming sexual compulsivity, "you have to make a habit"—reflecting what Matt calls "an active commitment to improve the areas that directly contribute to your porn habit."

Matt described how his recovery began to resemble more of a "personal development plan for a growth-minded, healthy person"—something that reflects "more of who you are becoming in your life, not just the behaviors you are avoiding." He notes that it's common for plans to be passive like, "I have this filtered, and I have this cut off, and I don't do this, and I don't do that." This kind of a "laundry list" of rigid rules has "no energy to it," Matt suggests. "We can't recover with just porn-avoiding strategies. Recovery is active. We need something to replace not only that time with, but the identity we relate to." This can include simple, strategic steps like Matt's commitment to "go to bed with [his] wife each night."

Roger describes, "[I] replaced my bad behavior with good behavior. I started running, roller-skating and scrapbooking. I connected with people more, and I practiced cautiousness when alone." Rather than just the addictive patterns itself directly changing, the *rest of his life* changed too—both as a protection and as another way to signal a heart truly committed.

"The year after, my life was different," says Eva, after making a new commitment to healing, "there was a process my life had to go through."

"[Establish] places away from technology to go when you are feeling the urge," Joshua says. "Go into public places and your neighborhoods; engage in the world around you. We live in a real world with real adventure. Don't just stay inside your home all weekend—take a walk under the stars."

Recovery Temperature Check: What's currently your weakest boundary or structural support? What specific adjustment would strengthen this vulnerable area?

Anti-addiction lifestyle challenge: Design your time and physical space in a way that makes sober living and freedom easier—making strategic adjustments day-by-day. Try to find whether there's a "keystone habit" in your day that ripples throughout the rest of the day (for instance, "if I get up early, then I'm able to exercise and get some meditation and prayer time, which infuses the rest of my day with good energy").

8. Learning to be consistent: Investing patiently in steady, daily efforts—rather than quick fixes—for lasting recovery.

"Too often, we see Impact Suite members who drop out because they 'couldn't wait for change.' They wanted it right now, in their way, on their terms," says Vinny, one of our main team members, with a decade of his own sobriety. "That patience is especially important during times where natural motivation, connection, and inspiration recede—or when withdrawal effects emerge. Without the numbing agents, there is more life to feel as well." He continues, "One of the signs that you are changing is that you have a sense of patience in your recovery process"—recognizing that "when it comes to real, lasting change there are no 'quick fixes' and being "willing to be patient and keep moving down your own personal path of change for as long as it takes."

In his first year of sobriety, Chris was surprised to discover, "I still had problems. I thought it was going to be heavenly that everything would go great, but it didn't." Yet he says, "I realized, well, I no longer have my drug of choice to numb out. And that's why I'm forced now to feel and process what I'm feeling."

"[Once people] stop all the self-protecting schemes," Nick says, some new discomfort is an "inevitable consequence."

Josh describes coming to understand these stretching moments as a chance for further growth, even though they "send [him] for a loop" and are "not fun."

Staying engaged daily.

Vinny speaks of being consistently engaged in the "daily routines" and "daily self-cares" that bring about real change. He describes the importance of "staying keenly interested, on a daily basis, in your recovery"—which he defines as "the aggressive pursuit of a great and happy life."

Roger came to see his recovery as a matter of life and death—both in securing his freedom and retaining it. "I know that if I do not want to destroy my body and die spiritually, I have to comply with my new life."

Stephen likewise speaks of the need to have "a willing heart to live in recovery. This must be my true desire. I must choose to be fully committed to the work of recovery with a humble attitude."

There's a sustaining power to simple practices like daily gratitude:

"Being thankful for the little things," as Josh says.

One religious man describes the added peace and joy that came from "a daily exercise to put on the full armor of God and to fill [his] life with things that invite the Holy Ghost."

Whatever it takes.

"When you're serious about changing unwanted behaviors," Vinny acknowledges, "you have a mindset that says, 'I will do whatever it takes to change'—a kind of "unconditional willingness" he contrasted with a "mindset of conditional change," aka, "I'll do anything to change so long as it doesn't involve [fill in the blank]."

"In my early years before I got really serious about my own recovery, I place[d] all kinds of conditions on my commitment to change," Vinny continues.

Rather than fear what others would think or financial consequences, he describes coming to a deeper *why*, saying, "I don't want to be a slave anymore. I want freedom to choose the direction of my life. I want to become the best man I can be and will *never* discover this with porn in my life. I want to discover real intimacy with my wife."

Not giving up after a setback.

When people find themselves "going back into the ditch," one man reminds, "That is not the end of the world."

"I still slipped. I still fell. But I'd learned that it was a journey and not a light switch," Tony says, adding that "a fall does not negate all of the progress that went before it."

Chris says that even when he fell, he had the feeling of "get back up, you can do this." He continues, "And I hope everyone who struggles with some form of addiction gets that feeling. . . . The truth is we will fall. We all do." But referencing how he sees his higher power, he says, "he's there lovingly, lifting us up and helping us. Back on that path to grab hold and to go a few more steps forward. And there's no one saying, Well, sorry you reach your quota, your limit is up.'"

After a profound moment of learning, Mark says, "I *wish I could tell you* that this is all it took for the scales to fall from my eyes. . . . I *wish I could tell you* that I walked out and never looked back."

> But he adds, "As is the case with many of us, we don't always learn the lesson the first time we hear it."

Others share similar language after what they thought were major turning points.

> After a sweet moment of inspiration, Jessica reflects, "I would *love to be able to say* that the next morning I woke up and had no recollection of the previous four years of addiction. I can't. The next morning, I still had the same flesh I had the day before. My body still craved that high. I had been in it so long that I felt sometimes I ran on autopilot. My mind would say, 'I'm not going to do that today,' but my feet would walk into the computer room and I would fall again."

> "When I got rid of the part of the cycle where I beat myself up, the cycle broke down," Thomas reflects—encouraging others: "One day, I decided that if I looked at porn, I wasn't going to beat myself up about it, I would pick up and move on." He continues: "You would not believe how fast porn faded from my life after years of addiction when I changed my outlook. Instead of letting the old tapes play in my head of, 'I'm a piece of crap who can't stop looking at smut,' I went with, 'I screwed up today, but God still loves me, and I'm gonna try to let that change me tomorrow, but if I don't, God will still love me tomorrow too.' When I got rid of the part of the cycle where I beat myself up, the cycle broke down."

However arduous, the length of the recovery process often teaches someone profound lessons about who we are and what is most important.

> **Recovery Temperature Check:** What's one recovery practice you've maintained consistently, and what factors have helped you sustain it? How might you apply those same factors to other areas where consistency has been challenging?

Anti-addiction lifestyle challenge: Think seriously about how to bring more stamina and resilience to your recovery plan overall, as well as to the smaller moments of your daily lifestyle that are easy to ignore and forget. Experiment with picking up a new consistency in the small and big parts of your healing journey, doing so in a way that generates positive recovery momentum over time.

9. Serving others: Turning attention outward by helping those in need and finding purpose beyond oneself.

Getting "outside of yourself" is a long-standing component of lasting recovery for many. One individual refers to Alcoholics Anonymous founder Bill W., who knew that he could not stay sober if he wasn't working with other alcoholics. This individual adds, "I have felt that in my own life, I will not be sober if I wasn't committed to working with other people because that work gives me strength, gives me hope, and I need that strength."

Service in recovery plays a special role in disrupting addiction's self-focused patterns. The most effective recovery service activities directly counteract addiction's core dynamics: replacing isolation with connection, secrecy with transparency, instant gratification with delayed reward, and self-focus with other-focus.

Living for others.

Nick was struck to see more clearly the "depth of [his] addiction to self and to feeling good," something that he realized his "whole life was centered around." Now looking back, he can see how he put his "wants and needs above those of everyone else."

"Our journey toward freedom" must become "one of serving and loving others," where we "remove ourselves from the center." Compared with "little boys" who "do what feels good, want it right now, and make life all about them," Nick says, "grown men" have "learned to wait, do what is right" and to "care about others."

Mark recounts how his "vocation as a husband and father" of four children helped him "stay pure," since he needed "all the graces he could receive" to be the father he needed to be.

"You will never experience ultimate and lasting freedom until this journey ceases to be about you and becomes all about others around you" Nick suggests. "This is rebirth," he says—"a new heaven, a new earth, and a new us!"

Reaching for others seeking freedom.

Several recovered individuals have gone on to facilitate programs supporting others in recovery.

"Once those chains are broken, you want to help everyone else find it," Eric says. "I began to make progress as I began to focus on others."

Jackson says, "I found in my heart a special place for those less fortunate than myself. As I helped them with their struggles, I found the power to face mine."

Others describe becoming more involved at church and helping family, with one man relating how he has been able to serve and love his wife more.

Recovery Temperature Check: How has your addiction caused you to prioritize your needs above others? What's one specific way you could begin reversing this pattern through service?

> **Anti-addiction lifestyle challenge:** Think of someone tonight who is facing something really difficult—someone who you could make a difference for by reaching out or serving in some way. Even if it's just a text, an email, or a phone call, make a plan and do it this week.

10. Exploring spirituality: Tapping into faith practices that provide comfort, strength, and a sense of identity.

There is a growing secular community of people seeking freedom from compulsive porn and masturbation. Yet many stories of people who have found deeper, more lasting freedom reflect a prioritization of spiritual matters, with one woman saying, "if you want true freedom, you have to care for your spirit and soul first."

Many experience spiritual healing through meditation, connecting with nature or animals, and volunteer opportunities, while others find a special boost in following traditional religious avenues.

> After struggling for so long, Mark recalls, "all I wanted to do was quench my impure sexual thirst, and it became a daily routine for me. [Yet] one spring day I decided to do something I hadn't done in a long time"—actively seeking to rekindle a relationship with God.

In some cases, gaining faith prompted some to realize what porn was really doing to them:

> "It was after I decided to become a Christian in my senior year of high school," Thomas says. "When I realized I should get rid of pornography in my life. Not because Jesus gets angry if I look

at porn, like some kind of angry jerk boss. Jesus is basically the opposite of that. He cares deeply for me and wants what's best for me. He is fighting on your behalf."

Finding spiritual support.

"If you feel humiliated and shameful for things of the past," one individual says, "just know God is very merciful and as you come to him, you are literally born again."

Abdul says, "As I began to focus on my relationship with Allah, and my Muslim faith, my recovery efforts seemed magnified and accelerated."

As Vinny observes, a "spiritual walk" is "accessible" to everyone—as people regain confidence in a "power greater than one's self."

One Jewish man who finally experienced lasting sobriety described "finding a real relationship with God and true serenity" through the 12-steps. "Just as God brought us out of Egypt at out lowest state of impurity," he writes, "so too He is the only One who can bring us out of our individual Egypt."[1]

"Ultimately, only God can set you free," Taylor insists. "Porn is not my savior. Jesus is my savior."

Nick Stumbo, a pastor who found lasting freedom, and Executive Director at Pure Desire Ministries, says, "Ultimately, you will have to find a new master"—describing what happens to those who "willingly chose to put their lives under the authority of another"—"contenting yourself in Him [and] trusting God beyond your own logic."

"The power to overcome does not lie within you alone," Jackson reiterates. "I spent more than a decade trying to overcome this on my own. Every time, I failed. Not until I reached the brink of destruction did I truly do what it really takes to overcome. I put my fate in God's hands."

Practicing spiritual patience.

Rather than a "quick" or "magic" process, Ken points out, "[It] usually doesn't work that way. It wasn't like I just cried out to the Lord once and I was free."

"Any relationship requires time and attention," another says.

Nick describes the impact of "reading His Word regularly, gathering weekly with other believers to hear and embrace truth, and submitting our will to Him daily through prayer."

Chantel noticed how many stories of lasting freedom involved fasting and prayer, which prompted her to do the same.

Austin spoke of making prayer "a very intentional thing—to be real with Jesus," saying, "I'm not going to put on a religious show."

A new source of comfort, love, and connection

More than simply an increase in power, people often speak of finding newfound comfort and love, as an upgrade from what porn had been offering.

"Porn can become our safe place, and when we need something, whether it's love, affirmation, or peace, we run to it," one said,

Another added, "Anytime I felt lacking, pornography was always there to buoy me up again."

Although repulsed by her first taste of pornography, Jessica admitted, "Something drew me in." Namely, "these women were being accepted."

Author Matt Dobschuetz reflects on "a porn star with sparkling eyes whose gaze would always make me feel seen," while remarking on the "ridiculous premises" of films "where I was the object of adoration, where I was wanted."[2]

It was the Dutch faith leader Henri Nouwen who taught that sexual brokenness "reveals to us our enormous yearning for communion, the desires of our body to be touched, embraced, and safely held"—which "belong to the deepest longings of our heart."

One man explains, "[My struggle had] a lot less to do with pornography and more to do with my emotions, my feelings, how I process those"—suggesting, "There really is strength and power in identifying what void am I trying to fill when I do that?"

Facing hard truths.

"Yeah, I was desperate [to change]," Josh says, "but the truth was, I wanted pornography—even though it was destroying my life." "[It's only] natural to pursue what we love," he adds. "The thing that was driving me in life was my desire for sexual pleasure—it was what I loved, thought about, and consumed."

Christian author John Bevere recollects asking in prayer, "God, you delivered my friend—I've been crying out. Why haven't you delivered me?" The answer: "Because you still like it." This prompted him to ask, "How can God deliver me from something I like and desire?"

"It is a heart issue," James says. "The reason I was going to pornography was that I was selfish."

Joshua agrees. "We are willing to get pleasure at the expense of others and use them as objects, not treating them as the human beings they are."

Loving something more than addiction

"As long as you pursue freedom from pornography," James suggests, "you'll never find freedom—freedom doesn't come from looking something in the eyes and saying, 'I better overcome that.' It comes from finding that which is more beautiful."

"I was pursuing freedom instead of pursuing Christ," one Christian man adds—describing how instead of waking up to focus on what it takes to find freedom, he now wakes up and seeks God's goodness and love in his life.

"Intimacy is what we seek, and an understanding of intimacy is what we lack," says Vinny—citing a therapist who once said, "I want to thank the porn industry today for teaching us absolutely *nothing* about true intimacy."

Another man speaks of feeling in prayer, "James, you want to stop the sin, the pain," but "you don't want a greater relationship to me. You don't want to be close to me." He continues, "When the battle changed from 'try to stop looking at porn'—to 'try to know God better,' suddenly victory was mine." At that point, James says, "Jesus was really able to begin doing some massive work in my life."

It was striking how many others share similar experiences:

"I had to first give my life to God," Chantel says. "You want him to be your one and only and you don't want *anything* to come between him and the relationship you are building with him."

"When I fell in love with Jesus, there was something that immediately, instinctively I knew *this is it*—this is going to be the thing that carries me." Austin recalls, "I'm going to have victory. That thing I was always seeking for—that void I was seeking inside, that I was trying to fill with love from other sources, now is filled with the love from Jesus."

"Make God your habit, and he'll break your habit," Pastor Jude Fouquier says. "Make God your addiction and you'll break your addiction."[3]

Not who I am.

Thomas, recalling a time when he was struggling to overcome, says,"I basically stopped fighting and just accepted that the addiction was part of who I am" and therefore, "I couldn't expect to behave any differently." Yet, he continues, "Every time I gave in to my addiction, it reinforced this idea and wrapped me tighter and tighter into my destructive behavior. It was my destiny."

"You know you're experiencing change when you're able to start seeing yourself outside of your behaviors," Vinny says—adding, "We are *not* our addiction." Many describe the impact of coming to see their own identity more completely.

"Finding true freedom is not just quitting a bad habit, it's about discovering the real you," Matt says.

Vinny describes taking "full responsibility" for his struggle, while also realizing that he had "great intrinsic worth and value that has nothing to do with addiction." He reflects, "We are *not* pieces of crap. We are not Evil. We are *not* freaks of nature. We are simply human beings with issues."

"I understood what it meant to have worth, true worth, not a sexual worth," Jessica recalls. "I realized that my body, with all of its quirks and inconsistencies, was fashioned exactly the way [God] planned, [and] my life was knit together and measured out to fulfill a purpose."

Austin likewise says, "my ultimate value is in [God]. I'm loved by him and I'm his child. He made me on purpose and I don't need to look anywhere else for that value."

Becoming what we love.

"We are all in the process of becoming," says Christian writer A.W. Tozer. "We have already moved from what we were to what we are, and we are now moving toward what we shall be. We are becoming what we love."

"What do we love?" Matt asks. "If we no longer are going to porn, where is our focus? What do we value?" He quotes another man who was "becoming the type of man that does not look at porn," instead of primarily "practicing behaviors that keep [him] from looking at porn." Matt says this was his singular "breakthrough," adding, "I'm a different person than I was when I was looking at porn every day."

Recovery Temperature Check: Does your recovery process include a spiritual foundation? How has addiction affected your sense of spiritual connection? What specific spiritual practice might help rebuild that connection?

Anti-addiction lifestyle challenge: Experiment with a spiritual practice others have found helpful in deepening their own sense of meaning, purpose, and identity. You might journal in a quiet place, meditate in nature, or try to pray (sharing openly what's on your heart, with as much faith as you can muster).

Additional Variables

Given the limitations of our methodology, it's worth pointing out here that there are at least three areas that figured prominently in our statistical analysis of healing and recovery from pornography addiction that didn't show up as frequently in these recovery narratives. These include:

1. **Physical wellness:** Compared with those who hadn't found freedom from pornography, a significantly greater percentage of people who find lasting freedom (between 21 percent and 29 percent more) told us they eat well and sleep well, with more modest differences in whether they are physically active and get regular sunlight.
2. **Mental wellness:** Those doing well in their sobriety also pay more attention to "what kind of news and entertainment media" they take into their mind (30 point spread), while limiting media making them "mad, sad or fearful" (12 points), along with 36 and 24 percentage point differences in whether they manage stress well and whether they regularly meditate, do yoga, or experience stillness in other ways (like art) to "help their mind rest."
3. **Broader healing from dependencies:** There was an especially significant 47 percentage point difference with people who found lasting freedom more likely to say they have "experienced healing from other compulsive patterns in my life (e.g., substance, media, spending)," and a smaller (10 and 13 percentage points) difference in whether they've "reduced

> dependence on alcohol or other recreational substances," and "tapered back on antidepressants, antianxiety drugs or other prescribed medication that was affecting [their] emotions."

Closing Reflections

It's been common in this project to pause in awe at what we're seeing—the beauty and marvel of it all. These stories of people who have found lasting healing and freedom are not fairy tales, though, and it's still important to appreciate some of the messier realities of what this looks like.

The recovery journeys documented here reveal a fundamental truth: Freedom isn't the absence of challenge but rather a transformed relationship with these many challenges. Rather than eliminating all challenging situations, these people developed a new response repertoire that allowed them to navigate previously overwhelming situations with growing confidence and capacity.

True freedom and healing doesn't mean you are no longer drawn to what you've left behind. James told us, "There are landmines all around me and every step counts. But I tell you, I am not what I used to be. I can't believe it!"

Never surrender. Stay hopeful. Keep believing. Keep connecting. Keep learning. And keep getting up! We'll be rooting for you.

Part III

How Can You Begin Your Own Healing Journey?

Chapter 7

Think Like a Mom

When you were a kid, who did you turn to when you were hurting? Who knew how to dry your tears, calm your worries, and make it all feel better? For many people, that source of comfort and gentle support came from Mom. Of course, some mother relationships are challenging and some can even be a source of harm. Still, motherhood at its best represents a gentle, loving, intuitive presence that comforts us like a warm embrace.

While traditional mothering is our primary metaphor here, the essence of healing and nurturing can come from many sources. Different cultures and families express care in unique ways through fathers, grandparents, chosen family, or community elders. The core elements—attentive presence, practical support, and tender patience—remain universal across these diverse expressions of care.

As we grow up, the challenges we face start to feel a whole lot more complicated, don't they? At this point, Band-Aids, chocolate chip cookies, and a kiss don't fix every hurt the way they used to. (Okay, a warm chocolate chip cookie *does* make the world seem like a brighter place!)

Even though there's no simple Band-Aid fix for depression, anxiety, addiction, or other struggles, there is still a lot of wisdom to be found in approaching these challenges with the same tender loving-kindness we associate with good mothers.

The Wisdom in a Mother's Approach to Illness

What did your mom or caretaker use to do when you got sick? Did she throw her hands up in the air, cry buckets of tears, and bemoan the fact that you had come down with the flu? Likely not. Hopefully, she instead said something like, "Let's get you a nice warm bath, some chicken noodle soup, extra blankets, and your fluffy pajamas."

That's what a good caretaker would say and do—boosting whatever support you needed to feel better, right?

And before you knew it, you *did* start to feel better.

That's because it doesn't typically take a back-breaking effort to overcome illness. Healing is what the body is designed to do. With a little extra support, physical symptoms like inflammation most often subside until we're well again.

So, you can see, all that "simple" stuff we do when we're sick is far more potent than we might think. In fact, those seemingly simple steps add up to a powerful, direct physiological intervention that helps to gradually move the body back to wholeness.

Ask yourself this: What if we approached a particularly dark or difficult episode of depression, anxiety, or some other emotional distress in a similar way? Rather than resigning ourselves to a lifelong ailment, considering a difficult experience as potentially changeable and healable—sort of like a case of the emotional flu?

Facing the Emotional Flu

For some, comparing mental health struggles to the flu might feel uncomfortable or even trivializing at first. After all, depression, anxiety, and other emotional challenges are often profound, complex experiences that can fundamentally shape our lives in ways that physical illness rarely does. None of this is to suggest these struggles are simple or brief, nor that everyone will recover quickly with some rest and with some soup (in fact, it's moving the body around and getting more actively involved in other people's lives that helps many).

What we are suggesting is a shift in how we think about these challenges, overall—and as you'll see, there are compelling reasons to consider this perspective. Rather than avoiding or procrastinating important changes, this is about allowing emotional pain to accentuate the importance of key adjustments.

It's fair to say this really isn't how most of us think about emotional problems. Many of us were taught that mental illness is a lifelong and chronic condition caused by underlying, enduring, even permanent biological problems.

Is that what you've heard too? It reflects what brain scientists *used* to believe was true.

Not anymore. Rather than a sad story of lifelong deficiency and struggle, it's remarkable how hopeful modern biological science really is with brain changeability, genetic fluidity, and new research pointing to a major biological contributor to depression.

Another Biological Contribution to Emotional Struggle

Inflammation. That's right! The same bodily response we know is connected to other kinds of physical illness. To go deeper, check out "The Inflamed Mind"[1] and "Brain Inflamed."[2]

Continuing the transformation of our understanding of mental health—sparked by new neuroscience—studies published in journals like *JAMA Psychiatry* and *Nature Neuroscience* have documented strong connections between inflammatory markers and depression. Researchers have found that people with depression often have elevated levels of inflammatory cytokines (proteins used by the immune system that help control inflammation) like IL-6 and TNF-alpha. Among other things, such inflammation can disrupt neurotransmitter function and neural circuits involved in mood regulation.

What's especially promising is that this inflammation responds to many of the same supportive interventions we instinctively use for physical illness: rest, nourishing food, gentle movement, and a calm environment. What we once thought of as merely self-care actually addresses biological mechanisms directly involved in both physical and mental health.

As you can see, unlike that older belief in a permanent biological defect, this kind of inflammation is modifiable—something we can work at and improve. Instead of a chronic condition to manage and endure, this approach to emotional challenges injects fresh hope at what may be possible.

Treating the Emotional Flu

Bringing to mind a time when you were struggling emotionally, consider the following questions:

- How could you adjust your normal life during this time of unique emotional distress? What would you eat, or not eat? How much would you rest and push back from normal responsibilities, at least for a time?
- What else would you do to pamper yourself a little, both emotionally and physically speaking? From blankets, slippers, teas, warm baths, saunas, and massage, to favorite movies, books, music, people, sunlight, and gentle movement. What might help?
- What have you done in the past that has lifted, soothed, and settled you emotionally? Can you incorporate more of those elements into your days the next time you are struggling? Is there anything you can adjust in your life to alleviate discomfort or suffering *right now*?

Consider Maria's experience: She noticed her anxiety increasing as work deadlines loomed. Instead of pushing through as usual, she remembered the "emotional flu" approach. She cleared her weekend calendar, prepared nourishing soups, gathered her softest blankets, and turned her phone to silent except for close family. She alternated between doing gentle yoga, reading uplifting poetry, and simply resting with her favorite herbal tea. By Sunday evening, the knot in her chest had loosened. While not completely resolved, her anxiety had become manageable enough that she could approach her upcoming work on Monday with new emotional reserves and a clearer mind.

Even the Body Can Change

This all might seem like a lot to adjust. But just think: What if it actually made a difference—helping restore your mind and body alike to a more settled, calm place? It's hard to put an exact time frame on healing, but it doesn't always have to take an extended amount of time either.

Especially as you bring careful attention to the variety of lifestyle adjustments that can make a difference, you'll almost inevitably start to feel a little better. That might be just a little at first, but it can pick up some momentum and grow into an "upward spiral" over time.

None of this, of course, means painful emotions will suddenly or quickly go away. Sometimes they can hang around, even for a long time—and even at intense levels. Give this gentle healing period enough time and patience to do its work.

Some people may need to replenish and renew for much longer than others, needing only an occasional retreat. And some may be tempted to spend *too long* in a place of rest—not recognizing signs that they're ready to progress to other activities.

The point here is that the pain *doesn't* have to stick around permanently. Not when we give our body, heart, and mind what they need. So, ask yourself:

» Have you ever approached depression and anxiety in this parental sort of way—gently, with targeted adjustments to your self-care and lifestyle?

» If so, what have you done to "baby yourself" for a time—and what kinds of specific adjustments did you make? What was the end result of these focused, gentle efforts?

» If you haven't ever tried this, what kinds of strategic adjustments could you make in a future moment of emotional difficulty?

More Than Just Coping

You *really can* hope for something more than simply managing and coping with your struggles in the years ahead. Did you know that one of the most effective historical mental health approaches essentially took this same approach on a large scale? In the eighteenth century, a Quaker community in York, England, tried an experiment to help loved ones that were ailing emotionally.[3]

This groundbreaking institution was called "The Retreat at York," founded in 1796 by William Tuke. Unlike the harsh asylums of the time, which often used restraints and isolation, Tuke pioneered what he called "moral treatment"—treating patients with dignity in a peaceful environment.

These humble people took brothers and sisters who were hurting and surrounded them with soft music, uplifting reading, good food, warm company, and beautiful gardens.

Patients engaged in meaningful work, enjoyed the carefully designed grounds, and were treated as valued community members rather than inmates. The results were remarkable—their recovery rates far exceeded contemporary institutions, prompting similar experiments throughout Europe and America for generations to come.

And what happened next? People started feeling better and getting better—for good. Many people found difficult emotional episodes passing more quickly. They often found themselves in a genuinely better and more stable place within.

Would you like to learn how to foster that kind of healing environment—for yourself and people you love? Imagine what it could mean to apply a similar healing renovation within the walls of your own home?

Creating Sanctuary

Your first mission, if you choose to accept it, is to take steps to cultivate and strengthen your own living space to become a legitimate sanctuary where healing can happen. Do what you can to create conditions around you right now to foster healing, not just in your mind and heart but also in your body—clearing up inflammation that plays a direct role in mental distress.

Here's a framework to help you build your healing sanctuary.

Physical Environment:

» **Light:** Maximize natural light exposure during the day; use warm, dimmable lighting in the evening.

» **Sound:** Curate a playlist of calming music or nature sounds; consider a white noise machine for sleep.

» **Scent:** Incorporate calming essential oils like lavender or chamomile in diffusers.

» **Touch:** Add soft textures through blankets, pillows, and comfortable clothing.

Daily Rhythms:

» **Morning ritual:** Begin with gentle movement and natural light exposure.

» **Nutritional support:** Focus on anti-inflammatory foods like leafy greens, fatty fish, and berries.

» **Rest periods:** Schedule brief "sanctuary moments" throughout your day.

» **Evening wind-down:** Establish a consistent, screen-free routine before sleep.

Social Environment:

» **Healing connections:** Identify your "sanctuary people" who bring calm and support.

» **Healing boundaries:** Create boundaries with relationships that increase unhealthy levels of stress (which is different from challenges and discomfort arising naturally in everyday relationships).

» **Healing communication:** Consider how to communicate your needs during difficult emotional periods.

See what you can do to take steps to cultivate a sanctuary right where you are. Not away at a healing retreat in some exotic location. But right here. In your own home and life.

Overcoming Barriers to Self-Nurturing

Creating space for healing isn't always straightforward. If you can justify putting additional time and energy into your own needs, you might face practical constraints such as limited time or resources and internal obstacles like wondering if you deserve to focus on your own needs.

If financial resources are limited, focus on no-cost approaches like natural light exposure, mindful breathing, or free community resources. If time is scarce, even five-minute "sanctuary moments" can be beneficial.

For those struggling with feelings that they don't deserve this kind of time, space, and care, remember that nurturing yourself enhances your capacity to show up for others. Just as flight attendants remind us to put on our own oxygen masks first, caring for your own emotional health is a necessary foundation for supporting those around you.

As you create conditions of healing around you, that atmosphere will invite prompt shifts not just in your mind and heart but also in your body—helping to clear up the inflammation that plays a direct role in mental distress.

Whatever it takes, start building that in-home sanctuary—creating conditions to weather through your own bouts of emotional flu and emerging stronger and better for it.

Chapter 8

Put on Your Sherlock Hat

When we're in emotional pain, our nervous system often shifts into survival mode. This natural response has a crucial purpose when facing immediate danger, but it can get in the way when it becomes the long-term way in which we manage stress, sorrow, and anxiety.

It's only natural when faced with intense pain emotionally and mentally, by the way, to shift into a restricted place of "fight or flight," aka "survival mode," where attention narrows, pupils dilate, heart rate increases, muscles tense, blood vessels constrict, and blood rushes to the extremities—all in preparation to confront a mortal threat to your well-being.

Isn't that pretty much how most of us now approach serious emotional and behavioral problems—as major crises, four-alarm fires that call on an emergency-level, heightened state of response? In this way, we subtly encourage those suffering to say to themselves, "Hey, you should be in survival mode."

Sometimes that may be exactly what is needed, especially when someone is hurting so much that it really is a life-and-death situation. But in other cases, this emergency-stance can cover up and distract from other important things—starting with deeper questions about what's going on. And if we miss that kind of curiosity, we may well miss some of the most important ways we can respond.

What if instead of approaching emotional distress as an emergency to manage, we approached it as a mystery to solve?

What Would Sherlock Do?

Looking deeper into what's happening seems fairly mundane at first, maybe even boring. But failure to go far enough in their search is exactly where many people get tripped up. They don't even realize what they're missing.

Think about it—when was the last time you watched or read a good Sherlock Holmes story? Does this ace detective ever arrive on the scene agitated, terrified, or hysterical?

No way. He shows up with unflappable calm, head full of curiosity, and eyes searching for cues.

We need to do the same. Instead of seeing emotional pain as a panic-inducing crisis to manage or a fire to be stomped out, consider approaching your emotional pain the same way—calm, curious, and inquisitive:

» When did this start? What is contributing to it? How many pieces are there to this puzzle?
» Could this pain be like an alarm system, calling your attention to certain patterns in your life needing adjustment?
» And what about your past? Could this be less about what's *wrong* with you and more about *what's happened* to you?
» "The best detectives don't jump to conclusions," notes Dr. Lisa Feldman Barrett, neuroscientist and author of *How Emotions Are Made*. "They gather evidence methodically, considering multiple possibilities before forming a theory. We should approach our emotional experiences with the same careful attention."[1]
» "The determining factors of depression are oftentimes the little things that we are not even aware of," William

says—emphasizing how important it was to be aware of the range of influences on mood.

» "You have to look at it from every angle," Ashley says about her depression healing journey, "because the disease affects every single part of your life and the way you feel about it."

Getting at the Roots

How exactly to get in this kind of a reflective place isn't always so clear. In a heightened state of emotion, it can be hard to think clearly, since survival is our focus. So different creative ways to cool-down the fight-or-flight mode—from meditation and yoga to a head-clearing walk or prayer—can be invaluable in getting into a better head space where a difficult emotional or behavioral challenge can be examined, rather than only defended against.

Additional Emotional Regulation Tips:

Here are two quick grounding methods to use when overwhelmed with anxiety or emotional pain.

Box Breathing: Inhale through the nose for 4 seconds. Hold that breath for 4 seconds. Exhale slowly through the mouth for 4 seconds. Hold for 4 seconds. Repeat 4 times.

5-4-3-2-1 Method: Name 5 things you can see, 4 things you can touch, 3 things you can hear, 2 things you can smell, and 1 thing you can taste

It's the intensity of this emotional pain that has motivated so many people to search for answers—prompting literally tens of thousands of studies that examine hundreds of potential contributors to mental health and addiction challenges. This wide scientific interest is impressive, albeit quite a challenge, since the amount of research is overwhelming and impossible for any one person to wade through.

We've been lucky enough as a team to have the time to review a big chunk of the available research. And we're happy to be able to summarize in different ways what we've found so you can explore them for yourself. It's been surprising how broadly this research literature touches diverse aspects of our lives, yes, *all of life*!

For instance, research has identified numerous potential contributors to emotional distress, including:

» **Biological influences:** Inflammation, gut health, sleep quality, nutrition deficiencies

» **Environmental influences:** Exposure to nature, living conditions, noise/light pollution

» **Lifestyle influences:** Movement patterns, rest/activity balance, stress levels

» **Psychological influences:** Thought patterns, trauma responses, coping mechanisms

» **Social influences:** Relationship quality, community connection, social support

It might be easy to see this as bad news (the fact that there's so much influencing us and contributing to our emotional state). But it's really not—in fact, this is all super good news.

Because if there's a lot of things contributing, that means there's a lot of things you can do to move your life and emotional health in a better direction.

Once you've started looking at the wide variety of potential contributors to serious emotional pain, you can begin to personalize a deeper healing plan with much greater precision—that could include any short-term needs as well as what it will take to reach long-term healing.

When you orient your view beyond immediate symptom change alone, looking toward the big picture, you start to ask different questions and to draw different conclusions.

The Detective's Toolkit: Practical Investigation Skills

How can you develop your inner Sherlock? Here are some practical tools:

1. **The Emotional Journal:** Track your emotions, their intensity, and relevant circumstances over time to spot patterns. As part of this, you could take note of your "mental diet"—what you take into your mind on a daily and weekly basis.
2. **The Timeline Tool:** Map significant life events across time, comparing them with periods of emotional difficulty to identify connections. Are there any events in your school, work, or personal life that coincide with periods of anxiety or depression?
3. **The Body Scan:** Develop awareness of physical sensations that accompany emotional states. Develop awareness of physical sensations that accompany emotional states. In what ways does your anxiety or depression manifest physically? For instance, you might notice your anxiety is accompanied by a stomachache or a headache.
4. **Environmental Audit:** Assess how your surroundings might be affecting your well-being. Are there any changes you can make to your home or work environment to make the space more welcoming?
5. **Relationship Inventory:** Consider how your social connections influence your emotional health. How do you feel after spending time with certain people? Are there connections that energize or drain you?

Listening for the Nudge

Like all good mysteries, the puzzle gets solved one piece at a time. But you have to again be in a state ready for new learning and discoveries, allowing you to play the part of a scientist (or detective) in your own life.

With each clue, you can start to unravel the mystery in your actual life. But instead of trying to "figure it all out," be on the lookout for nudges confirming the *next right step*. What will that be for you?

Let's find out.

How long you spend exploring and investigating is totally up to you. It can be helpful to put some real time into this—but unhelpful if you end up pouring too much time into it (time that may be more effectively invested in action).

So, if you're spending weeks and weeks exploring why you're hurting, you might consider whether it's time to get moving. On the other end of the spectrum, some hardly take any time to think deeply about these questions. Trust your intuition to know what's best for you. We'd recommend taking at least a couple of days—or as long as a week or two—to really let yourself explore what's really going on inside.

Consider James's experience: After years of battling anxiety, he set aside a weekend for his own "Sherlock investigation." He created a timeline of when his anxiety had worsened or improved, kept notes on physical sensations that accompanied anxious episodes, and identified triggers in his environment. By Sunday evening, he had several promising clues to follow—including a possible connection between his caffeine consumption and anxiety spikes, as well as a pattern of anxiety following conversations with a particularly critical colleague.

If you're struggling to grasp the importance of getting curious and exploring more deeply what's happening, we'll now extend to you a cinematic prescription ("reel therapy" is a real thing![2]). Before moving on, pause long enough to watch one of the many great Sherlock Holmes movies—you need to feel this in your bones!

Hearing the Signal

As challenging as it may be at first, slowing down and letting yourself get a little more curious about what's going on inside opens up another stirring possibility: Instead of being so quick to run away from what hurts, you can start thinking about pain as a messenger.

In his best-selling book on depression, British journalist Johann Hari shares his own recovery experience before offering this counsel: "I know this is going to be hard to hear because I know how deep your suffering cuts. But this pain isn't your enemy, however much it hurts (oh goodness, I know how much it hurts). It's your ally—leading you away from [one life] and pointing the way toward a more fulfilling one."[3]

Rather than constantly resisting or fighting against the pain, the idea here is listening to it—to see what insights it has to offer about what changes we may need to make. Hari goes deeper:

> Your distress is a signal—a necessary signal. Instead of seeing your depression and anxiety as a form of madness, you need to see the sanity in this sadness. You need to see that it makes sense. Of course, it is excruciating. . . [who wouldn't dread that pain returning?]. But that doesn't mean the pain is insane or irrational. Depression and anxiety might, in one way, be the sanest reaction you have. It's a signal, saying—you shouldn't have to live this way, and if you aren't helped to find a better path, you will be missing out on so much that is best about being human.

How does that sit with you—thinking about the contours and patterns of your own pain (or that of loved ones) as signaling something important? What might it shift if we believed there was legitimate sanity in the sadness and meaningful discoveries in our discomfort?

Hari concludes with this invitation: "You are at a fork in the road now. You can try to muffle the signal. That will likely lead you to many years when the pain will persist. Or you can listen to the signal and let it guide you—away from the things that are hurting and draining you, and toward the things that will meet your true needs."

So, which fork in the road will you choose?

Practicing the Art of Investigation: A Weekly Check-In

Here's a simple weekly practice to develop your detective skills:

1. Set aside thirty minutes in a quiet space with a journal.
2. Begin with three deep breaths to center yourself.
3. Ask yourself these questions:
    - What patterns have I noticed in my emotions this week?
    - Where in my body do I feel tension or discomfort?
    - What situations have triggered strong emotional responses?
    - What experiences have I noticed giving me a sense of peace or well-being?
    - What's one small clue that I discovered this week?
4. Write without judgment, as if objectively collecting evidence (which you are!).
5. End by noting one small action you might take based on what you've learned during the week.

As a complement to your journaling, you can also fill out the "Daily Check-In" in the Impact Suite app that allows you to rate multiple lifestyle factors, alongside key outcomes.

The Case for a Gentle Approach to Pain

Ask yourself: Is it really best to approach emotional pain like a kind of crisis or emergency that must be dealt with through swift action and direct force? What would a more gentle, patient, non-reactive way look like?

"The mind doesn't like to be forced," writes Oxford researcher Mark Williams—"and if you try, you won't eventually like what happens."[4]

Instead of a crisis to fix—involving urgent efforts to make our feelings go away—many people are experimenting with this more gentle and gradual way to respond to depression, anxiety, and even addiction. Rather than trying to shove the pain away, they're finding out it really is possible to do something else. We can learn an entirely different approach—one that helps us *be with* emotional pain long enough to learn from it, to work through it in creative ways.

And yes, to get underneath it and unsettle its roots—so it doesn't stay around forever. If you want this kind of deeper healing though, you have to do something counterintuitive at first: *not* just fight emotional pain out of the gate. Instead of moving fast in some direction, this means *stopping* long enough to look honestly at what's happening. This is something Thomas McConkie calls a "radical act."[5]

What could you learn from this kind of deeper exploration? When you are struggling with your "go-to" way to manage distressing emotion, could this help you find an alternative?

By the way, this gentle approach doesn't mean passively accepting suffering—it means approaching any discomfort with the precision of a detective, rather than the panic of someone fleeing a fire. It means developing the courage to look closely at what hurts, trusting that understanding will ultimately lead to healing.

In fairness, this can all start to feel a little overwhelming when you begin to seriously explore the range of contributors to mental and behavioral health problems—especially since every single contributor to mental health corresponds to another adjustment we can make in our lives. But it's exactly that fact which leads to the next, most exciting chapter of all.

Chapter 9

Embarking on Your Own Healing Adventure

Every great story has a moment when the hero sets out on their journey. This is yours.

At this point we hope you've been able to benefit from a broader, deeper look at the various lifestyle factors contributing to the emotional struggles you or your loved ones are facing. We also hope you've practiced a gentle and nurturing response to yourself and your family as you've begun to establish and follow a more comprehensive plan for sustainable healing. These are the main two thrusts of the practical steps we've outlined so far:

» Rejuvenate and draw strength.
» Inquire and get curious.

You're really moving now! Standing on these important foundations, you're in a great place to ask the question, "Now what?"

There's obviously no secret ninja skill or potion to make our struggles *poof* away. But you already knew that. By now, you appreciate, better than most, how enduring and painful these struggles can be—and the deeper pursuit that must be undertaken to find healing.

Ultimately, we've found that our journey towards healing is just that: a journey. A quest even, for lasting healing and freedom from the underlying suffering that has haunted so many of our lives and families.

Replenishing Your Hope

This healing quest likely isn't something you're only starting now. We realize that. It's no doubt something you've already been on, maybe even for a long time. And you may feel some discouragement at how long things sometimes take—wondering how your own story could possibly end well when so much hurt has taken place? And how could *your* world somehow find its way back to sweetness?

These questions may not be easy to answer. They touch on some of the deepest questions that have occupied humanity for a long time, and no soundbite or slick marketing pitch can satisfy us or resolve them. Nor can any expert or professional with the right letters after their name provide a tidy answer on what your future may hold. Ultimately, these answers will be found within your own journey—not anyone else's grand adventure.

As researcher Brené Brown reminds us, "Hope is not an emotion" alone. "It's a cognitive process—a way of thinking about yourself and the world." Hope requires us to believe that things can be better, that we have agency in creating change, and that there are paths forward worth taking.

Are you open to viewing your experiences as a quest of healing? If you need a heroic boost to your spirits, go read or watch one of the great sagas that resonates with you, like *Lord of the Rings*, *Star Wars*, or *Harry Potter*. Find examples that steady your heart, inspire you, and remind you of what you're still capable of experiencing.

Creating a Plan

If any of this feels a little overwhelming—from the wide range of contributors, to the many possible steps you can take, don't get discouraged. Take a deep breath and start taking notes as you keep learning and going deeper into your observations.

You could ask yourself, what am I learning and noticing that feels especially relevant to my own struggle? What factors can help spark a more sustainable healing path in my own life? This more adventurous approach to healing requires careful attention and tender care.

Reflecting on the years she pursued healing, Jada Pinkett Smith, American actress, singer, and talk show host, spoke of realizing that "the mind and heart can be extremely delicate without the foundation of a formidable spirit." Explaining, "What I eat, what I watch on TV, what music I listen to, how I care for my body, my spiritual practice, what people I surround myself with, the amount of stress I allow, and so on . . . either contribute to or deteriorate my mental health." She added, "Mental health is a daily practice for me. It's a practice of deep self-love."

As a way to help keep things that will benefit your healing in order, it can be helpful to gather all the possible ideas and steps you are exploring into one place. Bring together everything you think may help you move towards deeper healing or more lasting freedom. We call this organized, personalized, strategic plan a "Wellness Plan" or a "Freedom Plan."[1]

This plan can be as simple as a piece of white paper with your ideas on it—maybe separating them into "short-term" and "long-term" plans. Then treat these as different repositories or "buckets" for all your best ideas and inspirations that come up. For instance, "getting outside on a walk really felt good—for the next week, I'm going to try to get outside more" (short-term plan). Or, "I can see how much learning to meditate might help me with this. Taking a class feels like too much right now, but I'd really like to plan on that in the future" (long-term plan).

When creating your Wellness Plan, consider the following:

1. **Assessment areas:**
   - » **Physical:** Sleep quality, nutrition, exercise, and specific symptoms

- **Environmental:** Home atmosphere, access to nature, daily surroundings
- **Emotional:** Predominant emotional patterns, emotional triggers, coping strategies
- **Social:** Supportive relationships, challenging relationships, community connections
- **Spiritual:** Practices that give meaning and connection to something larger than yourself

2. **Short-term strategies (daily or weekly practices):**
   - Morning routine elements
   - Evening wind-down practices
   - Small daily actions that support well-being
   - Crisis management tools
3. **Long-term vision:**
   - Imagining what healing might look like in six months
   - Supports and resources you might need over time
   - Plans that will take more time and milestones to celebrate along the way

Your wellness plan doesn't have to be all that grand and complicated.

Embracing the Adventure

In all this, remember that quests and adventures are marked by high stakes. Harrowing moments of difficulty. Great dramatic scenes of relief. Tears. And grand, high hopes.

Did you realize that you, yourself, are right now on such an adventure?

Most people aren't in that mindset, especially when it comes to addiction or mental health challenges. But if you take on this perspective, it can make quite a difference. Rather than an onerous, unending, pointless burden—like pushing a rock up the hill—this can remind you that *you really are going somewhere!* One step at a time.

In this way, you can move in the direction of deeper peace and joy, while demonstrating the heroism this turbulent life asks from all of us. Moment by moment, you can take the next right step that is in line with your deeper sense of what feels right and whatever larger plan feels best. But what happens when the next step leads to more struggle?

That's not a problem, because you see . . . when you're on a quest, setbacks and challenges aren't all that surprising or unexpected. In some ways, they make the eventual victory and progress even more meaningful. This is well illustrated in one of the greatest adventure stories of all time—*The Lord of the Rings*. After a fearful setback in the second film, the main character Frodo says in despair, "I can't do this Sam." In response, his trusted travel companion says,

> I know. It's all wrong. By rights we shouldn't even be here. But it's like in the great stories, Mr. Frodo. The ones that really mattered. Full of darkness and danger they were. And sometimes you didn't want to know the end. Because how could the end be happy? How could the world go back to the way it was when so much bad had happened? But in the end, it's only a passing thing, this shadow. Even darkness must pass. A new day will come. And when the sun shines, it will shine out the clearer.[2]

"Those were the stories that stayed with you," Sam says. And he's right. This unfolding healing saga you're in the middle of will stay with you too.

Why is it that these adventure stories resonate with us so deeply? Sam answers, "Folk in those stories had lots of chances of turning back, only they didn't. They kept going, because they were holding on to something. That there is some good in this world, and it's worth fighting for."[3]

What has been worth fighting for in your own life? What good things are you holding on to? What gives you reason to not give up or turn back, even when everything inside of you is tired or scared or discouraged?

We hope you will find answers to those questions, if you haven't yet (and soon)! Because it's not just two fictional hobbits who can get a boost from remembering that the "darkness must pass," and holding onto hope of seeing a "new day come" where the "sun shines out the clearer."

Consider Michael's story: After three years of debilitating depression following a career setback, he began viewing his recovery as a heroic journey. "Instead of seeing myself as broken, I started seeing myself as being tested, like in all the stories I loved as a kid," he explains. "Each small victory—getting out of bed, calling a friend, taking a walk—became not just a coping strategy but a battle won in my larger quest." This shift in perspective didn't eliminate his struggle, but it gave meaning to it. "The depression is still there some days, but now I face it differently. I'm the protagonist in my own story, not just a victim of my chemistry."

Finding Your Next Right Step

Please don't forget. We're *not* saying everything needs to change dramatically, all at once. In fact, we're not even saying *one* thing needs to change dramatically. Neuroscientist Alex Korb has outlined how small changes can start to unravel the emotional knot. From his book, *The Upward Spiral: Using Neuroscience to Reverse the Course of Depression, One Small Change at a Time*, Dr. Korb argues that in "complex systems like the brain, even a little shift can change the resonance of the whole system."[4]

Think about the weather, for instance: "You might have a forecast for rain, but then the wind changes direction, the humidity drops by just 1 percent, and the day is sunny instead." In a similar way, Dr. Korb argues that small life changes that help tune even "one [brain] circuit just a tiny bit" can make a surprising, ripple effect on our mood.

> For example, exercise changes the electrical activity in your brain during sleep, which then reduces anxiety, improves mood, and gives you more energy to exercise [and interact with others]. Similarly, expressing gratitude activates serotonin production, which improves your mood and allows

> you to overcome bad habits, giving you more to be grateful for. Any tiny change can be just the push your brain needs to start spiraling upward.

Isn't this good news? Even small adjustments to how we're living can get the ball rolling in a significant way! All this explains why it's so important to be patient in this process. Don't forget, rather than trying to figure it all out—*all at once*—maybe instead try focusing on taking the next right step. Recovery and healing happen "one day at a time."

Eventually, the vibrancy of your own life will start to reinforce all you've learned. "Happy people don't stick needles in our arms," says our friend Vinny.

Here are some small "next right steps" that have made a difference for others:

- » A 10-minute morning meditation or time of worship
- » A fifteen-minute walk outside, regardless of weather
- » Limiting news or social media consumption to specific times
- » Eating one additional serving of vegetables daily
- » Drinking an extra glass of water each day
- » Reaching out to one supportive person each week
- » Practicing five minutes of deep breathing when feeling overwhelmed
- » An evening or morning gratitude practice, where you write three to five moments of peace, joy, or things you appreciate each day.
- » A consistent bedtime ritual that begins thirty minutes before sleep

How able do you feel to practice this kind of patience in your healing journey? Even as you settle in for the longer journey, you might watch out for one small adjustment to consider this week. That could be a shift in what you eat, how much you move around, how much sun you get, what time you go to bed, what you put into your mind . . . whatever you feel good about trying!

Leaving the Future Open

The ultimate destination of your journey is unresolved and uncertain. How exactly this healing will unfold in your life is what you're about to discover. No one can predict the timing exactly, and maybe that's okay. In this great adventure you're on, it's okay to not know everything that's coming. Although challenging, this uncertainty is a natural part of any serious journey.

Among other things, this sets the stage for courage, faith, and plenty of growth. We also encourage you to be cautious when anticipating what exactly the future will hold. As one woman told us, "Never predict the recovery of another person."

Don't close down your options. Instead, leave things open—yes, open to the possibility that healing can go really well, sometimes even better than we expected (cue the climactic moments in our favorite superhero movies). This also means staying open to the possibility that we may face more surprising struggles and setbacks than expected along the way, like the monstrous spider Frodo encountered out of the blue on the road to Mordor.

For most people, by the way, both of those prospects turn out to be true on their healing journey. It's both harder than they realized and more encouraging than they could have imagined. That's not a bad combination. In fact, it's how *all* the great stories really go.

The concept of "post-traumatic growth" captures this paradox well. Psychologists Richard Tedeschi and Lawrence Calhoun, who coined the term, found that many people who face significant life challenges don't just recover—they experience profound positive changes in how they view themselves, their relationships, and their priorities.[5] This doesn't minimize any of the suffering or pain; rather, it just means that growth and pain can coexist on the same journey.

Relishing a New Moment

As a last thought, don't forget the incredible power and potential in this very moment. Even if it doesn't feel like the start of something new, and even if you've fallen back over again and again, that's okay. As best you can, turn your focus again to *this* new moment, and ask yourself what learning, growth, and possibility is available—here and now!

Right now, take a deep breath. Feel your feet on the ground. Notice one thing you can see, one thing you can hear, and one thing you can feel. This moment—this exact moment—contains the possibility of a new beginning. Your healing adventure continues, one breath at a time.

Chapter 10

Finding Your Upward Spiral

We've offered plenty of encouragement and suggestions in this short volume about how to find deeper healing and freedom in your own life and family. But as a reminder, we're not making any of this up. The evidence speaks for itself.

What we've shared are conclusions derived from many stories of people who have *actually* gotten better. These incredible stories are bolstered by literally thousands of risk factors and intervention studies that back up the wisdom of these same lifestyle improvements reflected in their accounts.

Spiraling Upward

As a reminder, none of this means anyone needs to change *everything* about their life—and certainly not typically in a dramatic fashion. And to remind you, changes in one area can also be expected to spark changes in another. One research team describes this as an "upward spiral," something we saw evidence of repeatedly.[1] For instance, after Brooke stopped drinking, she describes immediately noticing that she couldn't tolerate the same kinds of guys she had been dating without the numbing agent accompanying them. After spending more time in stillness, she says, "slowly, meditation seduces me," to the point that she realizes:

> I don't want to settle for little moments of physical pleasure, distractions, and escapes. My spiritual birthright is far more blissful than this shadow dance: another pretty, oblivious man in my bed, another round of drinks, another concert to drown out the sound of the primal music inside of me.

Jacob once visited with a family whose depressed teenager felt unable to commit to anything except getting a little more sunshine. After two weeks of getting outside more to play sports with his father, this young man felt enough energy to experiment with adjustments to his diet, which triggered other improvements in a new momentum of expanding healing.

We described earlier how Thomas intentionally adjusted what he took into his mind in the evening: "I started to be choosier about what I watched, and who I hung out with because I had a really clear sense of how it was affecting me." He also took more time "digesting that intake," by including about twenty minutes of breathing and "calming exercises before bedtime, so that [his] body was actually going into rest—a deeper rest than [he] had known before. . . . And that created this virtuous cycle of resting more." Thomas continues, "I realized I felt really good when I exercised. And I noticed what foods made me feel good and what foods made me feel sick."

He describes these changes as having a "domino effect that started with this tiny bit of awareness that cascaded into other fortunate turnarounds." This kind of rippling effect shows up often in stories of deep healing.

Caleb likewise describes gradually making adjustments to his lifestyle, saying, "So every day I woke up with a little more energy—and reinvested that energy in the rest of my life." Talking about these cumulative adjustments, he says, "It all worked together," to the point of "triggering an upward spiral of recovery."

This concept of the upward spiral appears not only in personal stories but in research as well. Psychologist Barbara Fredrickson's "broaden-and-build" theory explains how positive emotions expand our repertoire of thoughts immediately available to our awareness.[2] This prompts new experiences that build skills and resources, which in turn create more positive emotions—a virtuous cycle that continues to spiral upward.

So many of these kinds of changes described above happen one at a time—unfolding as gradual, incremental, and cumulative adjustments that add up until they multiply quickly.

Still, it can be easy to think that every adjustment only adds a little—with progress *only* happening slowly. This isn't the case. As we saw in many accounts, *one* particular physical, mental, social, or spiritual adjustment can sometimes unleash the floodgates of healing with exponential, compounding results—much like a financial investment that grows over time.

This kind of a "sudden gain" in different moments or areas has been associated across many studies with "short-term and long-term improvements in depression and anxiety."[3] For instance, Caleb reports feeling dramatically better after he stopped eating legumes. Everything he had been doing up to that point, like continuing to learn, serve in meaningful ways, and keeping his mind and brain free of any dependence, had been helpful, but it wasn't until this catalyzing puzzle piece fell into place that he started to truly feel better.

What might your catalyzing puzzle piece be? For some, it's addressing a previously unrecognized food sensitivity. For others, it's finding the right form of movement that brings joy rather than obligation. For still others, it's connecting with a community that can nourish and support them. The key is to remain open to discovering what that missing piece might be for you.

So, what's your upward spiral? And what is the next adjustment you need to make to move you one step closer to more lasting healing in your own life?

Don't Stop Hoping

As you've already seen, people on the path to finding this deeper, long-term healing can hardly help but share their encouragement for others to stay hopeful. Just as despair can spark despair, so also can hope spark hope. "Are you one of us?" a patient once asked Marsha Linehan, who once felt hopelessly ill in a psychiatric unit but later became a respected therapist and founder of dialectical behavior therapy (DBT). "Because if you are, it would give all of us so much hope." Offering advice that would apply to addiction, mental illness, and other difficult challenges, Michael, one of the men in our long-term study, says:

> If you are in the dumps about a mental illness, please do not give up. There is light at the end of the tunnel. I know it may seem hopeless at times—it may seem like a darkness that never ends. But you can get through it. In fact, you might just be at the beginning of the final corner before the road turns to health, freedom and happiness. Please, do not give up. You can do this.

Like Dr. Kelly Turner, the cancer researcher we met in chapter 4, we want to "collect as many cases of healing as possible" and then do what we can to connect those struggling with others who have healed. Linehan describes her motivation to "get out of hell and get others out." We, too, feel a desire to join what another person rightly called a "crusade of hope."

Seeing Pain as a Teacher

Along the way, of course, this pathway is not all hollyhocks and roses. One reason hope is so life-changing is that these journeys are fraught and rarely easy. Yet from a more hopeful perspective, even pain and discomfort itself can begin to feel purposeful.

"The mind-bending effects and the darkness of my depression were most certainly the hardest chapter of my life," one individual says. "It was a horrific and painful experience that I do not wish on anyone. Fighting that war inside your head every day is not a good place to be in." But this person went on to say, "Though you may not see it as such just yet, depression is an opportunity to restructure your life for the better. Depression is your body's healthy response to unhealthy circumstances. It's a signal for you to notice that something is terribly awry in your life and that it requires change or your mind and body will keep shutting down. It's an opportunity in disguise."

Author J. K. Rowling calls depression the "terrible place that allowed [her] to come back stronger." And Melissa Bernstein (from Melissa & Doug) describes how she "learned firsthand that darkness didn't have to emanate from darkness."[4] Mendek Rubin likewise asks, "Could it be that the suffering we endure on this planet is the very thing that forces us to raise ourselves to a higher state?"[5]

"We aren't meant to dwell in the dark," Tina Knowles Lawson writes in the preface to another in healing memoir.[6] "But darkness can be an indicator helping us to ask the tough questions and take one faithful step at a time toward being all God created us to be."

Douglas refers to something in chemistry called "spontaneous transformation" in which "open systems disintegrate into a state of "creative chaos" and after a time reorganize themselves at a higher level than before." That's why, he concludes, that "falling apart is not necessarily a bad thing," with "so-called breakdowns" potentially "a precursor to breakthroughs."

"Deaths can be followed by resurrections," he says, quoting researcher Julius Siegel who observed, "In a remarkable number of cases, those who have suffered and prevail find that after their ordeal they begin to operate at a higher level than ever before. The terrible experiences of our lives, despite the pain they bring, may become our redemption."

Juanita says, "I have felt that the depression that started all of this journey was absolutely the worst that could have happened to me. At times I have said I wouldn't wish it on my worst enemy. [Yet] the dark night was for me the beginning of freedom," she adds,[7] as something that "invites us to know and be fully known to ourselves and to know

God in ways that perhaps we had never imagined."

"I can feel God's love even here," she adds, describing her own experience like "a phoenix rising from the ashes." Juanita reflects further, "I had to descend all those days and nights into the darkness," or she wouldn't have learned important lessons. "This was about helping me build a life I wanted to live. The crash was not just about depression but about spiritual awakening, spiritual transformation."

William even claims, "Depression is the best thing that has ever happened to me."

This perspective—seeing suffering as potentially transformative—appears across many traditions and disciplines. The psychiatrist Viktor Frankl, who survived Nazi concentration camps, developed an entire therapeutic approach (logotherapy) based on finding meaning in suffering. The psychologist Carl Jung spoke of the "night sea journey," a descent into darkness that precedes psychological rebirth. Indigenous healing traditions often frame illness as an initiation that can lead to wisdom and even to becoming a healer oneself.

Embrace Your Part in the Healing

As you turn attention to your own circumstance, we encourage you to own your progress by taking control of your health and "following your intuition." Deeper healing isn't done *to* people—it more often seems to involve their active participation and a sense of ownership *in* healing.

After sharing his healing story, Jonathan says his experience "will hopefully let you see for yourself the false impression that you are somehow trapped forever" in emotional struggles—adding, "You have just convinced yourself that all hope is gone but it's not true." This lines up well with what we often tell people participating in our Impact Suite app: "Keep learning, keep growing, keep connecting, keep staying hopeful, and keep getting back up again!"

Consider creating a personal healing manifesto—a declaration of commitment to your own well-being. This might include a statement like:

- I deserve the time and resources needed for my healing.
- My healing journey benefits not just me but everyone in my life.
- I honor both my progress and my setbacks as part of the same path.
- I claim my right to define what healing means for me.

Keep At It

These changes don't typically come easily, suddenly, or dramatically. Moni says, "I know that healing is possible. We just have to be willing to do the hard work to get there." Another person speaks of believing "that almost everyone is capable of doing the same mental/emotional/spiritual work" to reach "real deep lasting authentic healing."

"Do you want that? You can get it," this individual says. "[But] you've got to work for it. It is so worth it. It takes time and isn't easy. But it works. And if you do the work I believe you will receive healing."

Even amidst difficult emotional problems, Juanita says, "We can learn to live into new realities that bring freedom" and gain growth and insight that are "worth the descent into hell."

"Never, in a million years, did I think I could climb out of the hole depression had buried me in," another individual says, before encouraging others: "*Force* yourself to get out of bed and do the work *every day*. No matter what. *You are worth the effort!*"

"I know that if I exercise I get the benefits of the endorphins and the serotonin boost," David says. "I know that if I get enough sleep, meditate, connect with good friends, eat a diet designed to maximize my physical and mental health, . . . I will continue to be free."

By moving towards the right set of targeted interventions, another person expressed confidence that "you can engineer happiness."

This means staying in the game when a downturn happens. In this part of the mural of deepening healing, we've described people making adjustments in diet, rest, physical activity, sunlight, the physical environment and schedule of their lives, and the basic amount of stress.

None of this reflects, for any of these individuals, some kind of linear march upward. Rather, there are starts and stops, ebbs and flows, and fits and turns on people's journeys of recovery.

All this happens gradually with "the positive reinforcement" of each change "continu[ing] to build and layer," as Mark points it, even as recovery "evolved and changed in unexpected ways." He goes on to say, "With time, and mistakes, and beautiful, rare victories, you learn, you grow, you spiral up. I'm grateful to have learned that from my worst moments. Otherwise, my best moments might have passed me by uncherished."

Struggle, then, can become viewed by many as an opportunity, not just a problem. As Mark adds, "I was beginning to consider setbacks as pivots to something else," which allowed him to even begin experiencing "a certain gratitude for [his] struggle."

Don't Pretend it's All on You

Matt reflects, "I do not know the magnitude or difficulty of anyone else's experience," and he has an appreciation that his journey isn't a "mirror image" for another—instead, he expresses hope that readers take away simply "an encouragement to keep trying and discovering."

Yet, these comprehensive efforts clearly don't have independent power on their own to lead people to a better place—with extreme behavior shifts sometimes exhausting people rather than moving them to deeper healing.

Wisdom, patience, compassion, and community help leaven the loaf of healing—as does faith in a power and love greater than self. Sooner or later, one day at a time—moment by moment—people find their way to deeper peace, happiness, and freedom once again.

And you can too.

Remember that healing is rarely a solo journey. Throughout history and across cultures, healing has been understood as a communal process. Whether it's a twelve-step group, a faith community, a therapy circle, family support, or a dedicated ally, we heal better together.

As we close this book, we invite you to imagine yourself five years from now looking back on this moment as the beginning of your healing journey—or as a significant turning point, if you're already on your way. What would that future self want you to know right now? What encouragement would he or she offer? What would they celebrate about the steps you're taking today?

Your upward spiral begins with a single step and continues with each choice, each moment of awareness, each act of self-compassion. The path is there before you. You've already begun.

References

Introduction

Alex Korb, *The Upward Spiral* (New Harbinger Publications, 2015).

Chapter 1

Thomas Samuel Kuhn, *The Structure of Scientific Revolutions* (University of Chicago Press, 1967).

1. Managing Depression in Clinical Practice (Springer London, 2010).
2. Dan Witters, "US Depression Rates Reach New Highs," *Gallup* May 17, 2023, https://news.gallup.com/poll/505745/depression-rates-reach-new-highs.aspx.
3. Jorge V. Verlenden, Ari Fodeman, Natalie Wilkins, et al., "Mental Health and Suicide Risk Among High School Students and Protective Factors — Youth Risk Behavior Survey, United States, 2023," *MMWR Supplement* 73: http://dx.doi.org/10.15585/mmwr.su7304a9U.S.
4. Edward L. Shieffelin, "The Cultural Analysis of Depressive Affect: An Example from New Guinea" in *Culture and Depression: Studies in the Anthropology and Cross-Cultural Psychiatry of Affect and Disorder*, ed. Arthur Kleinman and Byron Good (University of California Press, 1985), 101-133, https://doi.org/10.2307/jj.2711593.8.
5. Charles Keyes. "The Interpretive Basis of Depression" in *Culture and Depression: Studies in the Anthropology and Cross-Cultural Psychiatry of Affect and Disorder*, ed. Arthur Kleinman and Byron Good (University of California Press, 1985), 153–174, https://doi.org/10.2307/jj.2711593.10.
6. Ibid.
7. Anthony Stevens and John Price, *Evolutionary Psychiatry: A New Beginning* (Routledge, 2015).
8. Roy J. Shephard and Andris Rode, *The Health Consequences of 'Modernisation': Evidence from Circumpolar Peoples* (Cambridge University Press, 1996).

9. Brandon H. Hidaka, "Depression as a disease of modernity: explanations for increasing prevalence." *Journal of Affective Disorders* 140, no. 3 (2012): 205–214. https://doi:10.1016/j.jad.2011.12.036.
10. Stephen S. Ilardi, *The Depression Cure: The 6-Step Program to Beat Depression without Drugs* (Da Capo Lifelong Books, 2010).
11. Rita Mae Brown, *Sudden Death* (Bantam, 1984).
12. It's widely accepted that the initial response to something like an antidepressant is widely varied, typically with one third failing to respond, about another third experiencing some noticeable relief, and another subset feeling worse.
13. Philip Burgess, Jane Pirkis, Damien Jolley, Harvey Whiteford, and Shekhar Saxena, "Do Nations' Mental Health Policies, Programs and Legislation Influence Their Suicide Rates?" *The Australian and New Zealand Journal of Psychiatry* 38, (2004), https://doi.org/10.1080/j.1440-1614.2004.01484.x. This study across 100 countries found that policies designed to improve access to psychiatric medications were associated with a measurable worsening of suicide rates. "It is a concern," the researchers concluded, "that national mental health initiatives are associated with an increase in suicide rates."

Chapter 2

1. Jeffrey R. Lacasse and Jonathan Leo, "Serotonin and Depression: A Disconnect between the Advertisements and the Scientific Literature." *PLoS Med* 2, no. 12 (2005); Jonathan Leo and Jeffrey R. Lacasse, "The Media and the Chemical Imbalance Theory of Depression." (2008). https://doi.org/10.1007/s12115-007-9047-3; Jeffrey R. Lacasse and Jonathan Leo (2015). Antidepressants and the Chemical Imbalance Theory of Depression: A Reflection and Update on the Discourse. *The Behavior Therapist* 38, no. 7, 206–213; Benjamin Ang, Mark Horowitz, and Joanna Moncrieff, "Is the Chemical Imbalance an 'Urban Legend'? An Exploration of the Status of the Serotonin Theory of Depression in the Scientific Literature," *SSM—Mental Health* 2, (2022).
2. Martin Seligman, "Learned Helplessness." *Annual Review of Medicine*, 23 (1972), 407-12: https://doi.org/10.1146/annurev.me.23.020172.002203.
3. Jacob Hess, "'Prozac Saved My Life' vs. 'Prozac Ruined My Life': Investigating the Adoption, Constitution and Maintenance of Distinct Interpretations Associated with Depression and its Medical Treatment." (University of Illinois Urbana-Champaign, 2009): https://hdl.handle.net/2142/11307.

4. Joanna Moncrieff, Ruth E. Cooper, Tom Stockmann, Simone Amendola, Michael P. Hengartner, and Mark A. Horowitz, "The Serotonin Theory of Depression: A Systematic Umbrella Review of the Evidence," *Mol Psychiatry* 28, 3243–3256 (2023): https://doi.org/10.1038/s41380-022-01661-0.
5. Hans S. Schroder, Jordyn Tovey, Reni Forer, William Schultz, Elizabeth T. Kneeland, and Jason S. Moser, "Where Do 'Chemical Imbalance' Beliefs Come From? Evaluating the Impact of Different Sources," *Frontiers in Psychology* 15, (2025): https://doi.org/10.3389/fpsyg.2024.1469913.
6. B. J. Deacon and G. L. Baird, "The Chemical Imbalance Explanation of Depression: Reducing Blame at What Cost?" *Journal of Social and Clinical Psychology* 28, no. 4, (2022): 415–435, https://doi.org/10.1521/jscp.2009.28.4.415.
7. The Council of Sustainable Healing, "Lesson 2 of Mindweather 101." Produced by Jacob Hess, Thomas McConkie, and Patrick Jennings. Posted April 30, 2020, YouTube, https://youtu.be/jHeYZoGhXDs?si=AWgoFn-JsUPDrk1i.
8. Dr. Elisha Goldstein, *Uncovering Happiness: Overcoming Depression with Mindfulness and Self-Compassion* (Simon & Schuster UK, 2015).
9. M. B. Keller, P. W. Lavori, T. I. Mueller, et al., "Time to Recovery, Chronicity, and Levels of Psychopathology in Major Depression: A 5-Year Prospective Follow-Up of 431 Subjects," *Arch Gen Psychiatry* 49, no. 10, (1992): 809–816. This study found nearly one-half of all patients experiencing a major depressive episode had recovered within six months; by one year more than two-thirds; and by two years, 80 percent.
10. Jacob Z. Hess, "Does Your Depression Keep Getting Worse? This Might Be Why," *Public Square Magazine*, July 15, 2022.
11. Benedict Carey, "How to Quit Antidepressants: Very Slowly, Doctors Say," *The New York Times*, March 5, 2019.
12. Michel E. Addis and Christopher Martell, *Overcoming Depression One Step at a Time*, (New Harbinger Publications, 2004).
13. Steve Ilardi, *The Depression Cure* (Balance, 2010).
14. Milena Batanova, Richard Weissbourd, and Joseph McIntyre, "Loneliness in America: Just the Tip of the Iceberg?" Harvard Graduate School of Education, Making Caring Common, 2024.
15. MaryCarol R. Hunter, Brenda W. Gillespie, and Sophie Yu-Pu Chen, "Urban Nature Experiences Reduce Stress in the Context of Daily Life Based on Salivary Biomarkers," *Frontiers in Psychology* 10, 2019, https://doi.org/10.3389/fpsyg.2019.00722
16. Jeffrey M. Schwartz and Sharon Begley, *The Mind and the Brain* (AbeBooks, 2022).

17. Louann Brizendine, *The Female Brain* (Broadway Books, 2006).
18. Alex Korb, *The Upward Spiral* (New Harbinger Publications, 2015).
19. Johann Hari, *Lost Connections* (Bloomsbury USA, 2018).
20. Daniel Fisher, "Recovery from Schizophrenia: From Seclusion to Empowerment," *Medscape*, 2006.
21. Jon Kabat-Zinn, *The Mindful Way Through Depression* (The Guilford Press, 2007).

Chapter 3:

1. Vaishnavi Zotey, Amol Andhale, Tejas Shegekar, Anup Juganavar, and Vaishnavi Zotey, "Adaptive Neuroplasticity in Brain Injury Recovery: Strategies and Insights," *Cureus* 15, no. 9 (2023), doi:10.7759/cureus.45873.
2. Eleonora De Filippi, Anira Escrichs, Estela Càmara, et al., "Meditation-Induced Effects on Whole-Brain Structural and Effective Connectivity," *Brain Structure & Function* 227 no, 6 (2022), doi:10.1007/s00429-022-02496-9.
3. Andy Eugene and Jolanta Masiak, "The Neuroprotective Aspects of Sleep," *MEDtube Science* 3, no. 1 (2015): 35-40.
4. Fernando Gómez-Pinilla, "Brain Foods: The Effects of Nutrients on Brain Function," *Nature Reviews: Neuroscience* 9, no. 7 (2008): 568–578, doi:10.1038/nrn2421.
5. "Exercise May Be Just as Effective as Medication for Treating Major Depression," Duke University Medical Center (1999).
6. Felice N. Jacka, Adrienne O'Neil, Rachelle Opie, et al., "A Randomised Controlled Trial of Dietary Improvement for Adults with Major Depression (the 'SMILES' trial)," *BMC Medicine* 15, no. 23 (2017): https://doi.org/10.1186/s12916-017-0791-y.
7. "Mindfulness-Based Cognitive Therapy for Depression: Replication and Exploration of Differential Relapse Prevention Effects," *Journal of Consulting and Clinical Psychology* 17, no. 1 (2024) 31–40. doi:10.1037/0022-006X.72.1.31
8. Iyas Daghlas, Jacqueline M. Lane, and Richa Saxena, "Genetically Proxied Diurnal Preference, Sleep Timing, and Risk of Major Depressive Disorder," *JAMA Psychology* 78, vol. 8:903–910: doi.org/10.1001/jamapsychiatry.2021.0959.
9. Neil Nedley and Francisco E Ramirez, "Nedley Depression Hit Hypothesis: Identifying Depression and Its Causes," *American Journal of Lifestyle Medicine* 10, no. 6 (2016): 422-428, doi.org/10.1177/1559827614550779.

10. Steve Ilardi. *The Depression Cure* (Balance, 2010).
11. Ibid.
12. Check out https://impactsuite.com/ to see both individual and organizational resources available, along with web or app-based digital tools that can assist people in tracking lifestyle correlations to mental health outcomes in their lives.
13. Daniel Johnson, Sebastian Deterding, Kerri-Ann Kuhn, et al., "Gamification for Health and Wellbeing: A Systematic Review of the Literature," *Internet Interventions* 6: 89–106, https://doi.org/10.1016/j.invent.2016.10.002.
14. Ben Sawyer, as cited in "Gamification for Health and Well-Being."
15. T Miron-Shatz, M M Hansen, F J Grajales, F Martin-Sanchez, and P D Bamidis. "Social Media for the Promotion of Holistic Self-Participatory Care: An Evidence Based Approach. Contribution of the IMIA Social Media Working Group," *Yearbook of Medical Informatics* 8 (2013): 162–168.
16. Ibid.
17. Ibid.
18. Ibid.
19. "Are Workplace Health Promotion Programs Effective at Improving Presenteeism in Workers? A Systematic Review and Best Evidence Synthesis of the Literature," *BMC Public Health* 11, no. 1: 395, https://doi.org/10.1186/1471-2458-11-395.
20. Nancy L. Sin and Sonja Lyubomirsky. "Enhancing Well-Being and Alleviating Depressive Symptoms with Positive Psychology Interventions: A Practice-Friendly Meta-Analysis," *Journal of Clinical Psychology* 65, no. 5: 467–487, https://doi.org/10.1002/jclp.20593.
21. Thomas L Webb, Judith Joseph, Lucy Yardley, and Susan Michie. "Using the Internet to Promote Health Behavior Change," *Journal of Medical Internet Research* 12, no. 1, doi:10.2196/jmir.1376.
22. Joseph Grenney, *Influencer: The Power to Change Anything* (McGraw-Hill Education, 2007).
23. Felice N. Jacka, Adrienne O'Neil, Rachelle Opie, et al., "A Randomised Controlled Trial of Dietary Improvement for Adults with Major Depression (the 'SMILES' trial)," *BMC Medicine* 15, no. 23 (2017): https://doi.org/10.1186/s12916-017-0791-y.
24. Roger Walsh, "Lifestyle and Mental Health," *American Psychologist* 66, no. 7 (2011): 579–592, https://doi.org/10.1037/a0021769.
25. Ibid.

Chapter 4

1. Kelly A. Turner. *Radical Remission* (HarperCollins, 2014).
2. As cited in Jo Nash, "The 5 Founding Fathers and A History of Positive Psychology," February 12, 2015.
3. C M Harding, G W Brooks, T Ashikaga, J S Strauss, and A Breier, "The Vermont longitudinal study of persons with severe mental illness, I: Methodology, study sample, and overall status 32 years later." *American Journal of Psychiatry* 144, no. 6 (1987): 718-26, doi.org/10.1176/ajp.144.6.718.
4. Mary Leamy, Victoria Bird, Clair Le Boutillier, Julie Williams, and Mike Slade. "Conceptual framework for personal recovery in mental health: systematic review and narrative synthesis," *British Journal of Psychiatry* 199, no. 6 (2011): 445–452.

Chapter 5

1. Mendek Rubin, *Quest for Eternal Sunshine: A Holocaust Survivor's Journey from Darkness to Light* (She Writes Press, 2020).
2. Although anxiety shows up in many depression narratives, stories that center exclusively around anxiety will be reported separately in a future analysis.
3. Johann Hari, *Lost Connections: Uncovering the Real Causes of Depression—and the Unexpected Solutions* (Bloomsbury, 2018).
4. Melissa Bernstein. *LifeLines: An Inspirational Journey from Profound Darkness to Radiant Light* (LifeLines, LLC, 2021)
5. Alexi Pappas, from interview by Sarah Yang, "This Olympian Is on a Mission to Make Mental Health a Priority in Sports," *WhoWhatWear*, January 20, 2021, https://www.whowhatwear.com/alexi-pappas-interview.
6. Melissa Bernstein. *LifeLines: An Inspirational Journey from Profound Darkness to Radiant Light* (LifeLines, LLC, 2021)
7. Viktor Frankl. *Man's Search for Meaning*, 1946.
8. Grace Witter. "Finding My Way Back to Myself from Depression," October 18, 2020.
9. Kylie Ora Lobell. "How Judaism Took Me Out of My Depression," *Aish*, 2026.

Chapter 6

1. Eliyahu Norstein, "My Exodus from Porn Addiction," *Aish*, 2026.
2. Grace Witter, "Finding My Way Back to Myself from Depression," October 18, 2020.

2. Matt Dobschuetz *Porn Free: Becoming the Type of Man That Does Not Look at Porn* (Two Falls Publishing, 2022).
3. Jude Fouquier, "Make God your addiction and He'll break your addiction", *YouTube*, uploaded by CityChurchCalifornia, January 31, 2023.

Chapter 7

1. Edward Bullmore, *The Inflamed Mind: A Radical New Approach to Depression* (Picador: 2019).
2. Kenneth Bock, *Brain Inflamed: Uncovering the Hidden Causes of Anxiety, Depression, and Other Mood Disorders in Adolescents and Teens* (HarperCollins, 2021).
3. "Robert Whitaker, "A Historical Example of Sustainable Healing," YouTube, uploaded by The Council for Sustainable Healing, January 2, 2018.

Chapter 8

1. Lisa Feldman Barrett, *How Emotions Are Made* (Houghton Mifflin Harcourt, 2017).
2. Gary Soloman, *Reel Therapy: How Movies Inspire You to Overcome Life's Problems* (Aslan Pub, 2001).
3. Johann Hari, *Lost Connections: Uncovering the Real Causes of Depression—and the Unexpected Solutions* (Bloomsbury, 2018).
4. Mark Williams, *The Mindful Way Through Depression: Freeing Yourself from Chronic Unhappiness* (The Guilford Press, 2007).
5. "The Radical Act." YouTube, uploaded by The Council for Sustainable Healing, May 6, 2014.

Chapter 9

1. Mary Ellen Copeland, *Wellness Recovery Action Plan* (Peach Press, 2011).
2. *The Lord of the Rings: The Two Towers*, directed by Peter Jackson (Burbank, CA: New Line Cinema, 2003).
3. Ibid.
4. Alex Korb, *The Upward Spiral* (New Harbinger Publications, 2015).
5. Richard Tedeschi and Lawrence Calhoun, *Trauma & Transformation: Growing in the Aftermath of Suffering* (Sage Publications, 1995).

Chapter 10

1. T Z Tang and R J DeRubeis, "Sudden Gains and Critical Sessions in Cognitive-Behavioral Therapy for Depression," *Journal of Consulting*

and Clinical Psychology 67, no. 6 (1999): 894–904, https://doi.org/10.1037//0022-006x.67.6.894.

2. Barbara Fredrickson, "The Broaden-and-Build Theory of Positive Emotions," *Royal Society of London* 359, no. 1449 (2004): 1367–1378, https://doi.org/10.1098/rstb.2004.1512.
3. Idan M Aderka, Angela Nickerson, Hans Jakob Bøe, and Stefan G Hofmann, "Sudden Gains During Psychological Treatments of Anxiety and Depression: A Meta-Analysis," *Journal of Consulting and Clinical Psychology* 80, no. 1 (2012): 93–103, https://doi.org/10.1037/a0026455.
4. Melissa Bernstein, *LifeLines: An Inspirational Journey from Profound Darkness to Radiant Light* (LifeLines, LLC, 2021).
5. Mendek Rubin *Quest for Eternal Sunshine: A Holocaust Survivor's Journey from Darkness to Light* (She Writes Press, 2020).
6. Tina Knowles Lawson, "Foreword" from Juanita Campbell Rasmus, *Learning to Be: Finding Your Center After the Bottom Falls Out* (IVP: 2020).
7. Referring to the fifteenth century leader, St. John of the Cross, who wrote about the "dark night of the soul."

Acknowledgments

There have been a lot of great people involved in the process of writing this book. We are grateful for all your support. First and foremost, we want to thank Jen and Monique, our wives, for their many years of trust, patience, and support.

We are grateful for our many team members at Fortify and Impact Suite over the years who have helped us create technology that reflects the vision outlined in the book. We know the hours and dedication you all put into creating tools that can change lives. Thank you.

A special thanks to Sam and Kacie Malouf. We are grateful for your hearts, your wisdom, and your consistent desire to make the world a better place.

It takes a lot of work and some incredible people to help turn our thoughts, research, and data into this book. Thanks to Lorelle Frank and Christian Lippert for feedback and writing support on earlier drafts of material. Thank you Debbie Lathrop for reviewing some of the recovery memories we've analyzed. And finally, thank you Diana Gourley and Kylee Shields for your skilled and wise editing support.

About Clay Olsen

Clay Olsen is a social entrepreneur and leader in mental health advocacy and digital wellness innovation. As CEO and Founder of Impact Suite, he has created award-winning self-care apps that have helped hundreds of thousands of individuals across more than 150 countries find lasting recovery from depression, anxiety, and addiction. He also serves as Chairman of the Board and Co-Founder of PHASE Alliance (Prevention and Healing Against Sexual Exploitation) that unites organizations and community leaders to combat sexual exploitation and trafficking.

In 2009, Clay cofounded Fight the New Drug, a science-based movement addressing the harms of pornography that has reached millions around the globe and has been featured on ABC, *The New York Times*, NPR, CBS, CNN, and *USA Today*. Clay's expertise has taken him to prestigious platforms worldwide, including the United Nations, Carnegie Mellon University, and the World Congress of Families. In 2015, he was asked to join the Top Youth Speakers National Speakers Association, and in 2017, received the "Visionary Leadership Award" from the National Center on Sexual Exploitation. Later, he received Utah's 40 Under 40 Award.

About Jacob Hess

Jacob Hess, PhD, is a community psychologist, mindfulness teacher, and reporter at *Deseret News*. With a doctorate from the University of Illinois, Urbana-Champaign, Jacob has dedicated his career to exploring conflicting sociopolitical and mental narratives in a way that invites more dialogue and understanding across difference.

Jacob's doctoral dissertation research focused on competing narratives of depression treatment, examining how different stories about mental illness shape therapeutic approaches.

As co-developer of Impact Suite's mindfulness-based digital tools, Jacob has helped translate complex psychological research into accessible resources for individuals facing depression, anxiety, and addiction, bridging the gap between academic understanding and real-world application.

Jacob is also the author of several influential books on mindfulness and spiritual practice, including *The Power of Stillness: Mindful Living for Latter-day Saints* and *The Practice of Stillness* (co-authored with Carrie Skarda). These works reflect his understanding of contemplative practices and their role in emotional healing—insights that inform the approaches featured throughout this book.

He lives in Paradise, Utah, with his wife Monique and their four sons and one daughter.

About Impact Suite

Impact Suite provides science-backed digital solutions that help transform lives through therapeutic lifestyle changes. Our approach is proven to help anyone seeking to improve their quality of life—particularly those facing depression, anxiety, chemical dependency, or sexual compulsivity.

This guide distills the core principles behind our award-winning platform, where small, targeted adjustments in key lifestyle areas lead to lasting positive change. The strategies within these pages complement the personalized support available through the Impact Suite App, where you'll find an ecosystem of tools designed for your specific wellness journey.

Our comprehensive platform combines professional teletherapy, science-backed education, precise pattern-tracking tools, supportive community, AI coaching, and access to certified specialists—all working together to help you achieve deeper healing and sustainable growth. This powerful combination has transformed tens of thousands of lives across hundreds of countries, and we're committed to making these resources accessible to everyone.

Ready to begin your journey? Download the Impact Suite app by scanning the QR code below:

ImpactSuite.com

About Familius

Visit Our Website: www.familius.com

Familius is a global trade publishing company that publishes books and other content to help families be happy. We believe that happy families are key to a better society and the foundation of a happy life. The greatest work anyone will ever do will be within the walls of their own home. And we don't mean vacuuming! We recognize that every family looks different and passionately believe in helping all families find greater joy, whatever their situation. To that end, we publish beautiful books that help families live our 10 Habits of Happy Family Life: *love together, play together, learn together, work together, talk together, heal together, read together, eat together, give together,* and *laugh together*. Further, Familius does not discriminate on the basis of race, color, religion, gender, age, nationality, disability, caste, or sexual orientation in any of its activities or operations. Founded in 2012, Familius is located in Sanger, California.

Connect

Facebook: www.facebook.com/familiusbooks
Pinterest: www.pinterest.com/familiusbooks
Instagram: @FamiliusBooks
TikTok: @FamiliusBooks

The most important work you ever do will be within the walls of your own home.